EUTHYPHRO,

APOLOGY, CRITO

PHAEDO *The Death Scene*

PLATO

Translated by
F. J. CHURCH

Translation revised, with an introduction, by
ROBERT D. CUMMING

EUTHYPHRO, APOLOGY, CRITO

CONTENTS
· · · · · · · · · · · · · · · ·

INTRODUCTION

THE TRIAL AND DEATH OF SOCRATES

I

The dialogues printed in this volume come at the beginning of the platonic corpus in its traditional arrangement. They have thus entered the European philosophical tradition as an appropriate introduction to Plato's thought. But they can also be read as an introduction to this tradition itself. For "the safest general characterization of the European philosophical tradition," according to Alfred North Whitehead, "is that it consists of a series of footnotes to Plato."

If this continuing series of footnotes still made Plato's philosophy available to us, we might be spared the effort of reading these dialogues. But these dialogues themselves imply that tradition may not be an entirely satisfactory vehicle for Plato's philosophy. Their narration of Socrates' trial and death exhibits a conflict between this philosophy and the traditions of the earliest society—fifth-century Athens—which we would today acknowledge as European, in recognition of its enlightened political and cultural behavior. Moreover, it is not a series of footnotes that Socrates is anticipating when he faces his condemnation by Athenian democracy and announces, "There is no prospect that I shall be the last victim."

We should, therefore, when we read these dialogues, attempt to explain the occurrence of the conflict between Plato's philosophy and the traditions of his society (and, to some extent perhaps, of our society), the fact that the conflict does not remain a harmless intellectual debate, and the particular role Socrates as an individual plays in the exposition of this philosophy and in the development of this conflict. Before we turn to the dialogues themselves for more detailed explanations, some preliminary suggestions may be helpful.

II

The philosophy which brings Socrates into conflict with society takes the form of dialogues. This conversational form is not a literary whim of Plato but represents his recognition that this philosophy is itself a social undertaking. A problem in this philosophy does not corner an individual and leave him to his own private resources; it requires conversational treatment because its implications can only be exposed by his taking into account other points of view besides his own. Hence Socrates reports at his trial that he cannot avoid occasions of social conflict, by refraining from his cross-examination of others, without abandoning philosophy itself.

When Socrates invites someone to participate in these philosophical conversations, he sometimes stresses their social character by commenting on a maxim which he coins from Homer: " 'When two go together, one sees before the other,' for all men are then more resourceful in action, statement, and thought." The dialogues in their written form broaden the social scope of this philosophy by inviting the reader in turn to introduce his own point of view into the conversation. To continue the conversation in this way is not to continue a tradition by appending a footnote, since the resources which the participant must bring with him are his actions as well as his statements and thoughts. In these dialogues the personal style of thought of each participant is not only displayed by his statements, but is also dramatized by the way in which the different participants come upon the problem at some moment when their lives overlap, as a consequence of the course of action to which each is committed. For example, in the first of the dialogues printed here, the problem is to determine what piety is, but the problem is encountered when Euthyphro encounters Socrates, and their paths cross because Euthyphro is on his way to accuse his father of impiety and Socrates is himself about to come up for his own trial on this same accusation.

Thus Plato employs the dialogue not just as a conversational form of philosophy but also as a dramatic form of philosophy. On the one hand, the individual's own point of view on a problem only emerges as it comes into conflict with the points of view expressed by the other individuals participating in the dialogue. On the other hand, each participant expresses his point of view as it merges with the moral character he manifests in his actions, so that the conflict does not remain merely verbal and intellectual. The drama of these dialogues is this movement of a problem through different minds and into different lives. The participants are at cross-purposes and collide because the point of view each states is not something he happens to have thought about; it is the direction in which the life he has been leading points. At his trial Socrates, therefore, distinguishes philosophy from the verbal facility of contemporary intellectuals—the so-called "sophists"—and his defense of the philosophic method of cross-examination is not that an unexamined statement may be fallacious but that "an unexamined life is not worth living."

If Socrates himself as an individual plays a pivotal role in this dramatic movement of a problem into different lives, it is because his cross-examination of others' lives is also his self-examination of his own life. Although Plato illustrates the social character of his philosophy by populating his dialogues with a broad sample of representatives of his society, he does not assume that the simple addition of their points of view would itself be the attainment of philosophic knowledge. It would merely reproduce the haphazard process by which social prejudices accumulate and incoherent traditions are established. The philosophic control which Plato exercises in binding different points of view together is largely achieved through Socrates' resistance to their limitations and removal of their distortions. When Socrates intervenes in these conversations, he is able to reverse the direction that the other participants lend to the examination of a problem, since he is an individual of exceptional moral integrity, whose proclaimed knowledge is self-knowledge. And this claim, which Socrates makes at his trial, is itself one rendering of the way in which moral integrity is for Plato at once the support and the outcome of coherent knowledge.

III

Since knowledge is self-knowledge, the credentials of a participant to examine a problem come up for examination in Plato's dialogues as well as the problem itself. A coward, for example, could not be expected to know what courage is, since his own cowardice would distort his apprehension of the problem and encroach on his effort to obtain this knowledge. Euthyphro finds himself entangled in this epistemological snare in the first dialogue. By pretending to reliable knowledge of religious tradition, he justifies his action of bringing an accusation of impiety against his father, who had neglected a laborer and had disavowed responsibility for his negligence. Socrates disturbs Euthyphro's complacency not only by showing that the religious tradition itself is incoherent, but also by raising the question of the integrity of Euthyphro's own action. The breadth of this question is obscured in translation by the narrowly religious meaning of the English expression "piety." Multiple translations, though too lax, might be more revealing—a sense of "obligation," of "responsibility," of "loyalty"—since religious piety for the Greeks enforced all the obligations that bind an individual to others, and engage his personal responsibility to his family and friends, and his political loyalty to the state and its traditions. Euthyphro concedes that Socrates' cross-examination has given a disturbing movement to their conversation: "But, Socrates, I really don't know how to explain to you what is in my mind. Whatever statement we put forward always somehow moves round in a circle, and will not stay where we put it" (p. 13). Socrates, however, renews the cross-examination in order to overcome Euthyphro's intellectual inertia and moral negligence and show that it is not just their statements but Euthyphro's mind that is being set in motion by their examination of piety, since piety itself involves the obligation to examine and take responsibility for one's own actions. Euthyphro himself has turned around, when he hurries off at the end of the dialogue. His ignorance of the obligations of piety have been recognized to be his lack of intellectual initiative and neglect of his moral responsibility, which leave him open to the danger of himself committing an act of impiety by prosecuting his father for an act of impiety.

Socrates is left behind to meet the accusation of impiety in the *Apology*. His situation is thus the reverse of Euthyphro's, who dramatically has been his foil. At the same time the first dialogue now illustrates in retrospect Socrates' application, to the definition of piety, of the method of cross-examination which has actually led to his being accused of impiety and of corrupting others by his example. For Socrates' defense against this legal accusation is that it is mere pretense and that the actual prejudice and resentment toward him are due to his unremitting cross-examination of his fellow Athenians, which reveals that they do not know what they pretend to know. Their pretended knowledge of the obligations of piety is lack of self-knowledge, inasmuch as it is simply public opinion, which Socrates cannot cross-examine because it is anonymous. "I have . . . ," he explains, "simply to spar with shadows in my defense, and to put questions which there is no one to answer" (p. 23). Nonetheless the *Apology* remains a dialogue; the answers of public resentment are the shouts of the Athenians which continually threaten to interrupt Socrates' defense. Although the unexamined life may not be worth living, the fully examined life cannot be lived. Socrates is condemned to death for impiety because his cross-examinations disturb the intellectual inertia and moral complacency which seem to be indispensable to the consolidation of public opinion, and hence to the political stability of society.

Socrates, however, defends his cross-examinations as a pious obligation to the state which he cannot relinquish even under the pressure of public opinion. Just as the reversal in the previous dialogue was the turning of the accusation of impiety against Euthyphro, so Socrates now turns this accusation against the chief prosecutor; just as the accusation of impiety in the *Euthyphro* also turned against religious tradition, so it now also turns against public opinion. Public opinion is impious in that it ignores all obligations; it is politically as well as intellectually irresponsible. Athenian society has not actually attained political stability during Socrates' lifetime but has swung from a democratic to a totalitarian regime and back to a democratic regime. He has been threatened with reprisals for his unswerving refusal to align his own actions with these fluctuations. But his example has thereby supplied a definition of loyalty that has not elsewhere been available in Athenian political life. Athens has been on trial, and the unjust verdict condemning him is actually the self-condemnation of a corrupt society.

Nevertheless, piety is something more than this personal integrity. That the attempt to define piety which began in the *Euthyphro* is still being continued in the third dialogue, the *Crito*, is hinted by the personification of the laws of Athens as parents; that the attempt is undergoing a further reversal and broadening of its scope is suggested by the way these personified laws' cross-examination of Socrates takes the place of the anonymous shouts of public opinion in the *Apology*. In the first dialogue Socrates discounted Euthyphro's pretended knowledge of the obligations of religious law, in directing his attention to his more personal obligations to a parent; in the *Apology* Socrates discounted the legal pretenses of his trial as concealed political pressure, and addressed his final appeal to his own loyal friends. Now one of these friends, Crito, pleads with Socrates to recognize his responsibilities to his friends and as the father of a family by escaping from the Athenian prison. Socrates, however, recognizes that the parental authority of Athenian laws commands a higher loyalty. By escaping he would repudiate the legal verdict against him. But laws stabilize human expectations and thus not only are indispensable to the existence of any society but also have guided his own personal development as a member of a particular society. For him to frustrate the expectation that a legal verdict once reached—even though it is unjust—will be carried out, would therefore not only undermine the stability of Athenian society but also the integrity of his own life. Indeed, if Socrates weakened in this way the legal fabric of social life, he could legitimately be accused of disloyalty himself and of corrupting others by his example, so that the legal verdict condemning him in the *Apology* would become just in retrospect.

The fourth dialogue in this sequence is the *Phaedo*, and its report of Socrates' death has been included in the present volume. The scene is still, as in the *Crito*, the Athenian prison; yet the philosophic setting and the implications of Socrates' imprisonment and death have shifted. His death was viewed in the *Apology* by his fellow citizens as the effective way of interrupting philosophic activity, and was accepted by Socrates himself in the *Crito* as a legal decision which keeps him in prison. But his actual physical death will release him from the changing pressures of a corrupt society, and from the restrictions of human laws, by exposing him instead to the apparently universal laws of physical change and corruption. The final obligations of a philosophic life therefore require further examination. In the *Apology* Socrates defended himself against an accusation of impiously undertaking scientific investigations of the physical universe, by distinguishing the morally reliable knowledge of human nature which he obtained by examining himself and others. Although the proximity of his physical death in the *Phaedo* no longer permits him to maintain this distinction in its earlier form, the reversal lends universal breadth to his earlier examinations of the problem of piety and binds together the different perspectives of the previous dialogues. The moral integrity which he has displayed, in the face of pressures which blur self-knowledge and deflect responsibility, finally points toward his mind's emancipation from its physical imprisonment by his own body. For his self-confidence when confronted with death as a political threat, as a legal decision, and at last as a physical fact, now becomes his confidence in the dominant place of mind in the universe. But this confidence still proceeds from the knowledge that he is himself responsible for his actions. Could the investigation of physical causes provide a coherent view of the universe, as the scientists assumed with whom he was confused in the *Apology*, Socrates' actions would have been the effects of his physical instinct for survival; he would have escaped from the Athenian prison, and would now be walking

the streets of some other Greek city, pretending to be a free
man but actually imprisoned by his own body:

> I think that these muscles and bones would long since have
> been in Megara or Boeotia, impelled by their conviction as to
> what is best, if I had not thought it more just and honorable
> to submit to whatever punishment the state might decide
> rather than escape and run away. But to call these things
> causes is preposterous. If it were said that without bones and
> muscles and the other parts of my body I could not have done
> what I thought best, that would be true; but to say that
> they are the cause of what I do, and that in this way mind
> controls my actions, and yet not the choice of what is best,
> would be a very loose and negligent statement. . . . And so
> one thinker makes the earth stay in its place below the heavens
> by surrounding it with a vortex. Another supports it on a
> foundation of air as if it were a wide trough. But they never
> think of searching for a power which causes things to be
> arranged for the best, nor do they think that such a power
> has any divine force. They assume that they will find some
> Atlas stronger than this, more immortal and more able to
> hold the universe together, and they never recognize that it
> is this force of moral obligation which must really bind the
> universe together and secure its coherence.[1]

The final prison scene, which is included in this volume,
describes Socrates' body stiffening in death under the effects of
the hemlock. But the European philosophical tradition encour-
ages a further retrospect, to the extent that it does disclose—
as Whitehead suggests—the surviving influence and continuing
vitality of Plato's thought. For this continued effort of the
human mind to obtain a coherent view of the universe then
seems to have been at stake in Socrates' actions, resisting and
dominating social and physical change and corruption.

IV

A brief comment should be added regarding the more
modest obligations which must be met in translating Plato's
statements. Because of his influence on our philosophical tra-

[1] *Phaedo* 99a.

dition, there is considerable danger that many of his Greek expressions will sound technical and stilted in English. The translations in this volume are those of F. J. Church, which more successfully than others preserve something of the precise but easy simplicity of Plato's original language. Extensive revisions have been made on nearly every page. The important revisions are those designed to achieve closer accuracy of translation and, wherever possible, to render frequently-repeated Greek expressions by repeating the same English expressions. This latter aim is not an attitude of merely pedantic piety toward the Greek texts. Rather it is hoped that the resulting translations will oblige the reader to trace for himself the different implications which are introduced by the different ways Plato uses such recurrent expressions as "piety" and "justice" and their cognates. As I have attempted to indicate in this introduction, just as a single platonic dialogue brings more than one point of view to bear on the examination of a problem, so successive dialogues furnish supplementary perspectives for the examination of related problems. When, in their anxiety to provide a fluent translation, translators interpose various English expressions, in order to render the implications the same Greek expression successively acquires, they conceal from the reader the continued relevance which Plato may have attached to the earlier implications. In this way they risk loosening what he attempted to bind together in the original dialogues in order to assure the coherence of his philosophy.

ROBERT D. CUMMING

COLUMBIA UNIVERSITY
June, 1955

EUTHYPHRO

Euthyphro. What in the world are you doing here in the king's hall,[1] Socrates? Why have you left your haunts in the Lyceum? You surely cannot have a suit before him, as I have.

Socrates. The Athenians, Euthyphro, call it an indictment, not a suit.

Euth. What? Do you mean that someone is prosecuting you? I cannot believe that you are prosecuting anyone yourself.

Socr. Certainly I am not.

Euth. Then is someone prosecuting you?

Socr. Yes.

Euth. Who is he?

Socr. I scarcely know him myself, Euthyphro; I think he must be some unknown young man. His name, however, is Meletus, and his district Pitthis, if you can call to mind any Meletus of that district—a hook-nosed man with lanky hair and rather a scanty beard.

Euth. I don't know him, Socrates. But tell me, what is he prosecuting you for?

Socr. What for? Not on trivial grounds, I think. It is no small thing for so young a man to have formed an opinion on such an important matter. For he, he says, knows how the young are corrupted, and who are their corrupters. He must be a wise man who, observing my ignorance, is going to accuse me to the

St. I
p. 2

---

[1] The anachronistic title "king" was retained by the magistrate who had jurisdiction over crimes affecting the state religion.—Ed.

1

state, as his mother, of corrupting his friends. I think that he is the only one who begins at the right point in his political reforms; for his first care is to make the young men as good as possible, just as a good farmer will take care of his young

3 plants first, and, after he has done that, of the others. And so Meletus, I suppose, is first clearing us away who, as he says, corrupt the young men growing up; and then, when he has done that, of course he will turn his attention to the older men, and so become a very great public benefactor. Indeed, that is only what you would expect when he goes to work in this way.

II *Euth.* I hope it may be so, Socrates, but I fear the opposite. It seems to me that in trying to injure you, he is really setting to work by striking a blow at the foundation of the state. But how, tell me, does he say that you corrupt the youth?

Socr. In a way which sounds absurd at first, my friend. He says that I am a maker of gods; and so he is prosecuting me, he says, for inventing new gods and for not believing in the old ones.

Euth. I understand, Socrates. It is because you say that you always have a divine guide. So he is prosecuting you for introducing religious reforms; and he is going into court to arouse prejudice against you, knowing that the multitude are easily prejudiced about such matters. Why, they laugh even at me, as if I were out of my mind, when I talk about divine things in the assembly and tell them what is going to happen; and yet I have never foretold anything which has not come true. But they are resentful of all people like us. We must not worry about them; we must meet them boldly.

III *Socr.* My dear Euthyphro, their ridicule is not a very serious matter. The Athenians, it seems to me, may think a man to be clever without paying him much attention, so long as they do not think that he teaches his wisdom to others. But as soon as they think that he makes other people clever, they get angry, whether it be from resentment, as you say, or for some other reason.

Euth. I am not very anxious to test their attitude toward me in this matter.

Socr. No, perhaps they think that you are reserved, and that you are not anxious to teach your wisdom to others. But I fear that they may think that I am; for my love of men makes me talk to everyone whom I meet quite freely and unreservedly, and without payment. Indeed, if I could I would gladly pay people myself to listen to me. If then, as I said just now, they were only going to laugh at me, as you say they do at you, it would not be at all an unpleasant way of spending the day— to spend it in court, joking and laughing. But if they are going to be in earnest, then only prophets like you can tell where the matter will end.

Euth. Well, Socrates, I dare say that nothing will come of it. Very likely you will be successful in your trial, and I think that I shall be in mine.

Socr. And what is this suit of yours, Euthyphro? Are you IV suing, or being sued?

Euth. I am suing.

Socr. Whom?

Euth. A man whom people think I must be mad to prosecute. 4

Socr. What? Has he wings to fly away with?

Euth. He is far enough from flying; he is a very old man.

Socr. Who is he?

Euth. He is my father.

Socr. Your father, my good man?

Euth. He is indeed.

Socr. What are you prosecuting him for? What is the accusation?

Euth. Murder, Socrates.

Socr. Good heavens, Euthyphro! Surely the multitude are ignorant of what is right. I take it that it is not everyone who could rightly do what you are doing; only a man who was already well advanced in wisdom.

Euth. That is quite true, Socrates.

Socr. Was the man whom your father killed a relative of yours? But, of course, he was. You would never have prosecuted your father for the murder of a stranger?

Euth. You amuse me, Socrates. What difference does it make whether the murdered man were a relative or a stranger? The only question that you have to ask is, did the murderer kill justly or not? If justly, you must let him alone; if unjustly, you must indict him for murder, even though he share your hearth and sit at your table. The pollution is the same if you associate with such a man, knowing what he has done, without purifying yourself, and him too, by bringing him to justice. In the present case the murdered man was a poor laborer of mine, who worked for us on our farm in Naxos. While drunk he got angry with one of our slaves and killed him. My father therefore bound the man hand and foot and threw him into a ditch, while he sent to Athens to ask the priest what he should do. While the messenger was gone, he entirely neglected the man, thinking that he was a murderer, and that it would be no great matter, even if he were to die. And that was exactly what happened; hunger and cold and his bonds killed him before the messenger returned. And now my father and the rest of my family are indignant with me because I am prosecuting my father for the murder of this murderer. They assert that he did not kill the man at all; and they say that, even if he had killed him over and over again, the man himself was a murderer, and that I ought not to concern myself about such a person because it is impious for a son to prosecute his father for murder. So little, Socrates, do they know the divine law of piety and impiety.

Socr. And do you mean to say, Euthyphro, that you think that you understand divine things and piety and impiety so accurately that, in such a case as you have stated, you can bring your father to justice without fear that you yourself may be doing something impious?

Euth. If I did not understand all these matters accurately,
5   Socrates, I should not be worth much—Euthyphro would not be any better than other men.

V   *Socr.* Then, my dear Euthyphro, I cannot do better than become your pupil and challenge Meletus on this very point before the trial begins. I should say that I had always thought it very important to have knowledge about divine things; and that

now, when he says that I offend by speaking carelessly about
them, and by introducing reforms, I have become your pupil.
And I should say, "Meletus, if you acknowledge Euthyphro to be
wise in these matters and to hold the correct belief, then think
the same of me and do not put me on trial; but if you do not,
then bring a suit, not against me, but against my master, for
corrupting his elders—namely, myself whom he corrupts by his
teaching, and his own father whom he corrupts by admonishing
and punishing him." And if I did not succeed in persuading him
to release me from the suit or to indict you in my place, then I
could repeat my challenge in court.

Euth. Yes, by Zeus! Socrates, I think I should find out his
weak points if he were to try to indict me. I should have a good
deal to say about him in court long before I spoke about myself.

Socr. Yes, my dear friend, and knowing this I am anxious
to become your pupil. I see that Meletus here, and others too,
seem not to notice you at all, but he sees through me without
difficulty and at once prosecutes me for impiety. Now, therefore, please explain to me what you were so confident just now
that you knew. Tell me what are righteousness and sacrilege
with respect to murder and everything else. I suppose that piety
is the same in all actions, and that impiety is always the opposite of piety, and retains its identity, and that, as impiety, it
always has the same character, which will be found in whatever
is impious.

Euth. Certainly, Socrates, I suppose so.

Socr. Tell me, then, what is piety and what is impiety?   VI

Euth. Well, then, I say that piety means prosecuting the unjust individual who has committed murder or sacrilege, or any
other such crime, as I am doing now, whether he is your father
or your mother or whoever he is; and I say that impiety means
not prosecuting him. And observe, Socrates, I will give you a
clear proof, which I have already given to others, that it is so,
and that doing right means not letting off unpunished the sacrilegious man, whosoever he may be. Men hold Zeus to be the
best and the most just of the gods; and they admit that Zeus   6
bound his own father, Cronos, for wrongfully devouring his

children; and that Cronos, in his turn, castrated his father for similar reasons. And yet these same men are incensed with me because I proceed against my father for doing wrong. So, you see, they say one thing in the case of the gods and quite another in mine.

Socr. Is not that why I am being prosecuted, Euthyphro? I mean, because I find it hard to accept such stories people tell about the gods? I expect that I shall be found at fault because I doubt those stories. Now if you who understand all these matters so well agree in holding all those tales true, then I suppose that I must yield to your authority. What could I say when I admit myself that I know nothing about them? But tell me, in the name of friendship, do you really believe that these things have actually happened?

Euth. Yes, and more amazing things, too, Socrates, which the multitude do not know of.

Socr. Then you really believe that there is war among the gods, and bitter hatreds, and battles, such as the poets tell of, and which the great painters have depicted in our temples, notably in the pictures which cover the robe that is carried up to the Acropolis at the great Panathenaic festival? Are we to say that these things are true, Euthyphro?

Euth. Yes, Socrates, and more besides. As I was saying, I will report to you many other stories about divine matters, if you like, which I am sure will astonish you when you hear them.

VII   *Socr.* I dare say. You shall report them to me at your leisure another time. At present please try to give a more definite answer to the question which I asked you just now. What I asked you, my friend, was, What is piety? and you have not explained it to me to my satisfaction. You only tell me that what you are doing now, namely, prosecuting your father for murder, is a pious act.

Euth. Well, that is true, Socrates.

Socr. Very likely. But many other actions are pious, are they not, Euthyphro?

Euth. Certainly.

Socr. Remember, then, I did not ask you to tell me one or two of all the many pious actions that there are; I want to know what is characteristic of piety which makes all pious actions pious. You said, I think, that there is one characteristic which makes all pious actions pious, and another characteristic which makes all impious actions impious. Do you not remember?

Euth. I do.

Socr. Well, then, explain to me what is this characteristic, that I may have it to turn to, and to use as a standard whereby to judge your actions and those of other men, and be able to say that whatever action resembles it is pious, and whatever does not, is not pious.

Euth. Yes, I will tell you that if you wish, Socrates.

Socr. Certainly I do.

Euth. Well, then, what is pleasing to the gods is pious, and 7 what is not pleasing to them is impious.

Socr. Fine, Euthyphro. Now you have given me the answer that I wanted. Whether what you say is true, I do not know yet. But, of course, you will go on to prove that it is true.

Euth. Certainly.

Socr. Come, then, let us examine our statement. The things VIII and the men that are pleasing to the gods are pious, and the things and the men that are displeasing to the gods are impious. But piety and impiety are not the same; they are as opposite as possible—was not that what we said?

Euth. Certainly.

Socr. And it seems the appropriate statement?

Euth. Yes, Socrates, certainly.

Socr. Have we not also said, Euthyphro, that there are quarrels and disagreements and hatreds among the gods?

Euth. We have.

Socr. But what kind of disagreement, my friend, causes hatred and anger? Let us look at the matter thus. If you and I were to disagree as to whether one number were more than another, would that make us angry and enemies? Should we not settle such a dispute at once by counting?

Euth. Of course.

Socr. And if we were to disagree as to the relative size of two things, we should measure them and put an end to the disagreement at once, should we not?

Euth. Yes.

Socr. And should we not settle a question about the relative weight of two things by weighing them?

Euth. Of course.

Socr. Then what is the question which would make us angry and enemies if we disagreed about it, and could not come to a settlement? Perhaps you have not an answer ready; but listen to mine. Is it not the question of the just and unjust, of the honorable and the dishonorable, of the good and the bad? Is it not questions about these matters which make you and me and everyone else quarrel, when we do quarrel, if we differ about them and can reach no satisfactory agreement?

Euth. Yes, Socrates, it is disagreements about these matters.

Socr. Well, Euthyphro, the gods will quarrel over these things if they quarrel at all, will they not?

Euth. Necessarily.

Socr. Then, my good Euthyphro, you say that some of the gods think one thing just, the others another; and that what some of them hold to be honorable or good, others hold to be dishonorable or evil. For there would not have been quarrels among them if they had not disagreed on these points, would there?

Euth. You are right.

Socr. And each of them loves what he thinks honorable, and good, and just; and hates the opposite, does he not?

Euth. Certainly.

Socr. But you say that the same action is held by some of them to be just, and by others to be unjust; and that then they dispute about it, and so quarrel and fight among themselves. Is it not so?

Euth. Yes.

Socr. Then the same thing is hated by the gods and loved by them; and the same thing will be displeasing and pleasing to them.

Euth. Apparently.

Socr. Then, according to your account, the same thing will be pious and impious.

Euth. So it seems.

Socr. Then, my good friend, you have not answered my question. I did not ask you to tell me what action is both pious and impious; but it seems that whatever is pleasing to the gods is also displeasing to them. And so, Euthyphro, I should not be surprised if what you are doing now in punishing your father is an action well pleasing to Zeus, but hateful to Cronos and Uranus, and acceptable to Hephaestus, but hateful to Hera; and if any of the other gods disagree about it, pleasing to some of them and displeasing to others.

IX

Euth. But on this point, Socrates, I think that there is no difference of opinion among the gods: they all hold that if one man kills another unjustly, he must be punished.

Socr. What, Euthyphro? Among mankind, have you never heard disputes whether a man ought to be punished for killing another man unjustly, or for doing some other unjust deed?

Euth. Indeed, they never cease from these disputes, especially in courts of justice. They do all manner of unjust things; and then there is nothing which they will not do and say to avoid punishment.

Socr. Do they admit that they have done something unjust, and at the same time deny that they ought to be punished, Euthyphro?

Euth. No, indeed, that they do not.

Socr. Then it is not the case that there is nothing which they will not do and say. I take it, they do not dare to say or argue that they must not be punished if they have done something unjust. What they say is that they have not done anything unjust, is it not so?

Euth. That is true.

Socr. Then they do not disagree over the question that the unjust individual must be punished. They disagree over the question, who is unjust, and what was done and when, do they not?

Euth. That is true.

Socr. Well, is not exactly the same thing true of the gods if they quarrel about justice and injustice, as you say they do? Do not some of them say that the others are doing something unjust, while the others deny it? No one, I suppose, my dear friend, whether god or man, dares to say that a person who has done something unjust must not be punished.

Euth. No, Socrates, that is true, by and large.

Socr. I take it, Euthyphro, that the disputants, whether men or gods, if the gods do disagree, disagree over each separate act. When they quarrel about any act, some of them say that it was just, and others that it was unjust. Is it not so?

Euth. Yes.

X
9

Socr. Come, then, my dear Euthyphro, please enlighten me on this point. What proof have you that all the gods think that a laborer who has been imprisoned for murder by the master of the man whom he has murdered, and who dies from his imprisonment before the master has had time to learn from the religious authorities what he should do, dies unjustly? How do you know that it is just for a son to indict his father and to prosecute him for the murder of such a man? Come, see if you can make it clear to me that the gods necessarily agree in thinking that this action of yours is just; and if you satisfy me, I will never cease singing your praises for wisdom.

Euth. I could make that clear enough to you, Socrates; but I am afraid that it would be a long business.

Socr. I see you think that I am duller than the judges. To them, of course, you will make it clear that your father has committed an unjust action, and that all the gods agree in hating such actions.

Euth. I will indeed, Socrates, if they will only listen to me.

XI

Socr. They will listen if they think that you are a good speaker. But while you were talking, it occurred to me to ask myself this question: suppose that Euthyphro were to prove to me as clearly as possible that all the gods think such a death unjust, how has he brought me any nearer to understanding what piety and impiety are? This particular act, perhaps, may be displeasing to the gods, but then we have just seen that piety and impiety cannot be defined in that way; for we have seen that what is displeasing to the gods is also pleasing to them. So I will let you off on this point, Euthyphro; and all the gods shall agree in thinking your father's action wrong and in hating it, if you like. But shall we correct our definition and say that whatever all the gods hate is impious, and whatever they all love is pious; while whatever some of them love, and others hate, is either both or neither? Do you wish us now to define piety and impiety in this manner?

Euth. Why not, Socrates?

Socr. There is no reason why I should not, Euthyphro. It is for you to consider whether that definition will help you to teach me what you promised.

Euth. Well, I should say that piety is what all the gods love, and that impiety is what they all hate.

Socr. Are we to examine this definition, Euthyphro, and see if it is a good one? Or are we to be content to accept the bare statements of other men or of ourselves without asking any questions? Or must we examine the statements?

Euth. We must examine them. But for my part I think that the definition is right this time.

Socr. We shall know that better in a little while, my good XII friend. Now consider this question. Do the gods love piety 10 because it is pious, or is it pious because they love it?

Euth. I do not understand you, Socrates.

Socr. I will try to explain myself: we speak of a thing being carried and carrying, and being led and leading, and being seen and seeing; and you understand that all such expressions mean different things, and what the difference is.

Euth. Yes, I think I understand.

Socr. And we talk of a thing being loved, of a thing loving, and the two are different?

Euth. Of course.

Socr. Now tell me, is a thing which is being carried in a state of being carried because it is carried, or for some other reason?

Euth. No, because it is carried.

Socr. And a thing is in a state of being led because it is led, and of being seen because it is seen?

Euth. Certainly.

Socr. Then a thing is not seen because it is in a state of being seen: it is in a state of being seen because it is seen; and a thing is not led because it is in a state of being led: it is in a state of being led because it is led; and a thing is not carried because it is in a state of being carried: it is in a state of being carried because it is carried. Is my meaning clear now, Euthyphro? I mean this: if anything becomes or is affected, it does not become because it is in a state of becoming: it is in a state of becoming because it becomes; and it is not affected because it is in a state of being affected: it is in a state of being affected because it is affected. Do you not agree?

Euth. I do.

Socr. Is not that which is being loved in a state either of becoming or of being affected in some way by something?

Euth. Certainly.

Socr. Then the same is true here as in the former cases. A thing is not loved by those who love it because it is in a state of being loved; it is in a state of being loved because they love it.

Euth. Necessarily.

Socr. Well, then, Euthyphro, what do we say about piety? Is it not loved by all the gods, according to your definition?

Euth. Yes.

Socr. Because it is pious, or for some other reason?

Euth. No, because it is pious.

Socr. Then it is loved by the gods because it is pious; it is not pious because it is loved by them?

Euth. It seems so.

Socr. But, then, what is pleasing to the gods is pleasing to them, and is in a state of being loved by them, because they love it?

Euth. Of course.

Socr. Then piety is not what is pleasing to the gods, and what is pleasing to the gods is not pious, as you say, Euthyphro. They are different things.

Euth. And why, Socrates?

Socr. Because we are agreed that the gods love piety because it is pious, and that it is not pious because they love it. Is not this so?

Euth. Yes.

Socr. And that what is pleasing to the gods because they love it, is pleasing to them by reason of this same love, and that they do not love it because it is pleasing to them.   XIII

Euth. True.

Socr. Then, my dear Euthyphro, piety and what is pleasing to the gods are different things. If the gods had loved piety be-   11 cause it is pious, they would also have loved what is pleasing to them because it is pleasing to them; but if what is pleasing to them had been pleasing to them because they loved it, then piety, too, would have been piety because they loved it. But now you see that they are opposite things, and wholly different from each other. For the one is of a sort to be loved because it is loved, while the other is loved because it is of a sort to be loved. My question, Euthyphro, was, What is piety? But it turns out that you have not explained to me the essential character of piety; you have been content to mention an effect which belongs to it— namely, that all the gods love it. You have not yet told me what its essential character is. Do not, if you please, keep from me what piety is; begin again and tell me that. Never mind whether the gods love it, or whether it has other effects: we shall not differ on that point. Do your best to make clear to me what is piety and what is impiety.

Euth. But, Socrates, I really don't know how to explain to you what is in my mind. Whatever statement we put forward always somehow moves round in a circle, and will not stay where we put it.

Socr. I think that your statements, Euthyphro, are worthy of my ancestor Daedalus.[2] If they had been mine and I had set them down, I dare say you would have made fun of me, and said that it was the consequence of my descent from Daedalus

[2] Daedalus' statues were reputed to have been so lifelike that they came alive.—Ed.

that the statements which I construct run away, as his statues used to, and will not stay where they are put. But, as it is, the statements are yours, and the joke would have no point. You yourself see that they will not stay still.

Euth. Nay, Socrates, I think that the joke is very much in point. It is not my fault that the statement moves round in a circle and will not stay still. But you are the Daedalus, I think; as far as I am concerned, my statements would have stayed put.

Socr. Then, my friend, I must be a more skillful artist than Daedalus; he only used to make his own works move, while I, you see, can make other people's works move, too. And the beauty of it is that I am wise against my will. I would rather that our statements had remained firm and immovable than have all the wisdom of Daedalus and all the riches of Tantalus to boot. But enough of this. I will do my best to help you to explain to me what piety is, for I think that you are lazy. Don't give in yet. Tell me, do you not think that all piety must be just?

Euth. I do.

Socr. Well, then, is all justice pious, too? Or, while all
12 piety is just, is a part only of justice pious, and the rest of it something else?

Euth. I do not follow you, Socrates.

Socr. Yet you have the advantage over me in your youth no less than your wisdom. But, as I say, the wealth of your wisdom makes you complacent. Exert yourself, my good friend: I am not asking you a difficult question. I mean the opposite of what the poet [3] said, when he wrote:

"You shall not name Zeus the creator, who made all things: for where there is fear there also is reverence."

Now I disagree with the poet. Shall I tell you why?

Euth. Yes.

Socr. I do not think it true to say that where there is fear, there also is reverence. Many people who fear sickness and pov-

[3] Stasínus.

erty and other such evils seem to me to have fear, but no reverence for what they fear. Do you not think so?

Euth. I do.

Socr. But I think that where there is reverence there also
is fear. Does any man feel reverence and a sense of shame
about anything, without at the same time dreading and fearing
the reputation of wickedness?

Euth. No, certainly not.

Socr. Then, though there is fear wherever there is reverence, it is not correct to say that where there is fear there also
is reverence. Reverence does not always accompany fear; for
fear, I take it, is wider than reverence. It is a part of fear, just
as the odd is a part of number, so that where you have the odd
you must also have number, though where you have number
you do not necessarily have the odd. Now I think you follow
me?

Euth. I do.

Socr. Well, then, this is what I meant by the question which
I asked you. Is there always piety where there is justice? Or,
though there is always justice where there is piety, yet there
is not always piety where there is justice, because piety is only
a part of justice? Shall we say this, or do you differ?

Euth. No, I agree. I think that you are right.

Socr. Now observe the next point. If piety is a part of XIV
justice, we must find out, I suppose, what part of justice it is?
Now, if you had asked me just now, for instance, what part
of number is the odd, and what number is an odd number, I
should have said that whatever number is not even is an odd
number. Is it not so?

Euth. Yes.

Socr. Then see if you can explain to me what part of justice
is piety, that I may tell Meletus that now that I have been
adequately instructed by you as to what actions are righteous
and pious, and what are not, he must give up prosecuting me
unjustly for impiety.

Euth. Well, then, Socrates, I should say that righteousness
and piety are that part of justice which has to do with the

careful attention which ought to be paid to the gods; and that what has to do with the careful attention which ought to be paid to men is the remaining part of justice.

XV

13

Socr. And I think that your answer is a good one, Euthyphro. But there is one little point about which I still want to hear more. I do not yet understand what the careful attention is to which you refer. I suppose you do not mean that the attention which we pay to the gods is like the attention which we pay to other things. We say, for instance, do we not, that not everyone knows how to take care of horses, but only the trainer of horses?

Euth. Certainly.

Socr. For I suppose that the skill that is concerned with horses is the art of taking care of horses.

Euth. Yes.

Socr. And not everyone understands the care of dogs, but only the huntsman.

Euth. True.

Socr. For I suppose that the huntsman's skill is the art of taking care of dogs.

Euth. Yes.

Socr. And the herdsman's skill is the art of taking care of cattle.

Euth. Certainly.

Socr. And you say that piety and righteousness are taking care of the gods, Euthyphro?

Euth. I do.

Socr. Well, then, has not all care the same object? Is it not for the good and benefit of that on which it is bestowed? For instance, you see that horses are benefited and improved when they are cared for by the art which is concerned with them. Is it not so?

Euth. Yes, I think so.

Socr. And dogs are benefited and improved by the huntsman's art, and cattle by the herdsman's, are they not? And the same is always true. Or do you think care is ever meant to harm that which is cared for?

Euth. No, indeed; certainly not.

Socr. But to benefit it?

Euth. Of course.

Socr. Then is piety, which is our care for the gods, intended to benefit the gods, or to improve them? Should you allow that you make any of the gods better when you do a pious action?

Euth. No indeed; certainly not.

Socr. No, I am quite sure that that is not your meaning, Euthyphro. It was for that reason that I asked you what you meant by the careful attention which ought to be paid to the gods. I thought that you did not mean that.

Euth. You were right, Socrates. I do not mean that.

Socr. Good. Then what sort of attention to the gods will piety be?

Euth. The sort of attention, Socrates, slaves pay to their masters.

Socr. I understand; then it is a kind of service to the gods?

Euth. Certainly.

Socr. Can you tell me what result the art which serves XVI a doctor serves to produce? Is it not health?

Euth. Yes.

Socr. And what result does the art which serves a shipwright serve to produce?

Euth. A ship, of course, Socrates.

Socr. The result of the art which serves a builder is a house, is it not?

Euth. Yes.

Socr. Then tell me, my good friend: What result will the art which serves the gods serve to produce? You must know, seeing that you say that you know more about divine things than any other man.

Euth. Well, that is true, Socrates.

Socr. Then tell me, I beg you, what is that grand result which the gods use our services to produce?

Euth. There are many notable results, Socrates.

14 *Socr.* So are those, my friend, which a general produces. Yet it is easy to see that the crowning result of them all is victory in war, is it not?

Euth. Of course.

Socr. And, I take it, the farmer produces many notable results; yet the principal result of them all is that he makes the earth produce food.

Euth. Certainly.

Socr. Well, then, what is the principal result of the many notable results which the gods produce?

Euth. I told you just now, Socrates, that accurate knowledge of all these matters is not easily obtained. However, broadly I say this: if any man knows that his words and actions in prayer and sacrifice are acceptable to the gods, that is what is pious; and it preserves the state, as it does private families. But the opposite of what is acceptable to the gods is sacrilegious, and this it is that undermines and destroys everything.

XVII *Socr.* Certainly, Euthyphro, if you had wished, you could have answered my main question in far fewer words. But you are evidently not anxious to teach me. Just now, when you were on the very point of telling me what I want to know, you stopped short. If you had gone on then, I should have learned from you clearly enough by this time what piety is. But now I am asking you questions, and must follow wherever you lead me; so tell me, what is it that you mean by piety and impiety? Do you not mean a science of prayer and sacrifice?

Euth. I do.

Socr. To sacrifice is to give to the gods, and to pray is to ask of them, is it not?

Euth. It is, Socrates.

Socr. Then you say that piety is the science of asking of the gods and giving to them?

Euth. You understand my meaning exactly, Socrates.

Socr. Yes, for I am eager to share your wisdom, Euthyphro, and so I am all attention; nothing that you say will fall to the ground. But tell me, what is this service of the gods? You say it is to ask of them, and to give to them?

Euth. I do.

Socr. Then, to ask rightly will be to ask of them what we XVIII stand in need of from them, will it not?

Euth. Naturally.

Socr. And to give rightly will be to give back to them what they stand in need of from us? It would not be very skillful to make a present to a man of something that he has no need of.

Euth. True, Socrates.

Socr. Then piety, Euthyphro, will be the art of carrying on business between gods and men?

Euth. Yes, if you like to call it so.

Soc. But I like nothing except what is true. But tell me, how are the gods benefited by the gifts which they receive from us? What they give is plain enough. Every good thing that we have is their gift. But how are they benefited by what we 15 give them? Have we the advantage over them in these business transactions to such an extent that we receive from them all the good things we possess, and give them nothing in return?

Euth. But do you suppose, Socrates, that the gods are benefited by the gifts which they receive from us?

Socr. But what *are* these gifts, Euthyphro, that we give the gods?

Euth. What do you think but honor and praise, and, as I have said, what is acceptable to them.

Socr. Then piety, Euthyphro, is acceptable to the gods, but it is not profitable to them nor loved by them?

Euth. I think that nothing is more loved by them.

Socr. Then I see that piety means that which is loved by the gods.

Euth. Most certainly.

Socr. After that, shall you be surprised to find that your XIX statements move about instead of staying where you put them? Shall you accuse me of being the Daedalus that makes them move, when you yourself are far more skillful than Daedalus was, and make them go round in a circle? Do you not see that our statement has come round to where it was before? Surely you remember that we have already seen that piety and what is pleasing to the gods are quite different things. Do you not remember?

Euth. I do.

Socr. And now do you not see that you say that what the gods love is pious? But does not what the gods love come to the same thing as what is pleasing to the gods?

Euth. Certainly.

Socr. Then either our former conclusion was wrong or, if it was right, we are wrong now.

Euth. So it seems.

XX   *Socr.* Then we must begin again and inquire what piety is. I do not mean to give in until I have found out. Do not regard me as unworthy; give your whole mind to the question, and this time tell me the truth. For if anyone knows it, it is you; and you are a Proteus whom I must not let go until you have told me. It cannot be that you would ever have undertaken to prosecute your aged father for the murder of a laboring man unless you had known exactly what piety and impiety are. You would have feared to risk the anger of the gods, in case you should be doing wrong, and you would have been afraid of what men would say. But now I am sure that you think that you know exactly what is pious and what is not; so tell me, my good Euthyphro, and do not conceal from me what you think.

Euth. Another time, then, Socrates. I am in a hurry now, and it is time for me to be off.

Socr. What are you doing, my friend! Will you go away and destroy all my hopes of learning from you what is pious and what is not, and so of escaping Meletus? I meant to explain to him that now Euthyphro has made me wise about 16 divine things, and that I no longer in my ignorance speak carelessly about them or introduce reforms. And then I was going to promise him to live a better life for the future.

THE APOLOGY

CHARACTERS

SOCRATES

MELETUS

SCENE—The Court of Justice

Socrates. I do not know what impression my accusers have made upon you, Athenians. But I do know that they nearly made me forget who I was, so persuasive were they. And yet they have scarcely spoken one single word of truth. Of all their many falsehoods, the one which astonished me most was their saying that I was a clever speaker, and that you must be careful not to let me deceive you. I thought that it was most shameless of them not to be ashamed to talk in that way. For as soon as I open my mouth they will be refuted, and I shall prove that I am not a clever speaker in any way at all—unless, indeed, by a clever speaker they mean someone who speaks the truth. If that is their meaning, I agree with them that I am an orator not to be compared with them. My accusers, I repeat, have said little or nothing that is true, but from me you shall hear the whole truth. Certainly you will not hear a speech, Athenians, dressed up, like theirs, with fancy words and phrases. I will say to you what I have to say, without artifice, and I shall use the first words which come to mind, for I believe that what I have to say is just; so let none of you expect anything else. Indeed, my friends, it would hardly be right for me, at my age, to come before you like a schoolboy with his concocted phrases. But there is one thing, Athenians, which I do most earnestly beg and entreat of you. Do not be surprised and do not interrupt with shouts if in my defense I speak in the same way that I am accustomed to speak in the market place, at the tables of the money-changers,

21

where many of you have heard me, and elsewhere. The truth is this: I am more than seventy, and this is the first time that I have ever come before a law court; thus your manner of speech here is quite strange to me. If I had really been a stranger, you would have forgiven me for speaking in the language and the manner of my native country. And so now I ask you to grant me what I think I have a right to claim. Never mind the manner of my speech—it may be superior or it may be inferior to the usual manner. Give your whole attention to the question, whether what I say is just or not? That is what is required of a good judge, as speaking the truth is required of a good orator.

18

II   I have to defend myself, Athenians, first against the older false accusations of my old accusers, and then against the more recent ones of my present accusers. For many men have been accusing me to you, and for very many years, who have not spoken a word of truth; and I fear them more than I fear Anytus [1] and his associates, formidable as they are. But, my friends, the others are still more formidable, since they got hold of most of you when you were children and have been more persistent in accusing me untruthfully, persuading you that there is a certain Socrates, a wise man, who speculates about the heavens, who investigates things that are beneath the earth, and who can make the worse argument appear the stronger. These men, Athenians, who spread abroad this report are the accusers whom I fear; for their hearers think that persons who pursue such inquiries never believe in the gods. Besides they are many, their attacks have been going on for a long time, and they spoke to you when you were most ready to believe them, since you were all young, and some of you were children. And there was no one to answer them when they attacked me. The most preposterous thing of all is that I do not even know their names: I cannot tell you who they are except when one happens to be a comic poet. But all the rest who have persuaded

[1] Anytus is singled out as politically the most influential member of the prosecution. He had played a prominent part in the restoration of the democratic regime at Athens.—Ed.

you, from motives of resentment and prejudice, and sometimes, it may be, from conviction, are hardest to cope with. For I cannot call any one of them forward in court to cross-examine him. I have, as it were, simply to spar with shadows in my defense, and to put questions which there is no one to answer. I ask you, therefore, to believe that, as I say, I have been attacked by two kinds of accusers—first, by Meletus [2] and his associates, and, then, by those older ones of whom I have spoken. And, with your leave, I will defend myself first against my old accusers, since you heard their accusations first, and they were much more compelling than my present accusers are.

Well, I must make my defense, Athenians, and try in the short time allowed me to remove the prejudice which you have been so long a time acquiring. I hope that I may manage to do this, if it be best for you and for me, and that my defense may be successful; but I am quite aware of the nature of my task, and I know that it is a difficult one. Be the outcome, however, as is pleasing to god, I must obey the law and make my defense. **19**

Let us begin from the beginning, then, and ask what is the accusation that has given rise to the prejudice against me, on which Meletus relied when he brought his indictment. What is the prejudice which my enemies have been spreading about me? I must assume that they are formally accusing me, and read their indictment. It would run somewhat in this fashion: "Socrates is guilty of engaging in inquiries into things beneath the earth and in the heavens, of making the weaker argument appear the stronger, and of teaching others these same things." That is what they say. And in the comedy of Aristophanes [3] you yourselves saw a man called Socrates swinging **III**

[2] Apparently in order to obscure the political implications of the trial, the role of chief prosecutor was assigned to Meletus, a minor poet with fervent religious convictions. Anytus was evidently ready to make political use of Meletus' convictions without entirely sharing his fervor, for in the same year as this trial Meletus also prosecuted Andocides for impiety, but Anytus came to Andocides' defense.—Ed.

[3] *The Clouds.* The basket was satirically assumed to facilitate Socrates' inquiries into things in the heavens.—Ed.

around in a basket and saying that he walked on air, and sputtering a great deal of nonsense about matters of which I understand nothing at all. I do not mean to disparage that kind of knowledge if there is anyone who is wise about these matters. I trust Meletus may never be able to prosecute me for that. But the truth is, Athenians, I have nothing to do with these matters, and almost all of you are yourselves my witnesses of this. I beg all of you who have ever heard me discussing, and they are many, to inform your neighbors and tell them if any of you have ever heard me discussing such matters at all. That will show you that the other common statements about me are as false as this one.

IV 20 But the fact is that not one of these is true. And if you have heard that I undertake to educate men, and make money by so doing, that is not true either, though I think that it would be a fine thing to be able to educate men, as Gorgias of Leontini, and Prodicus of Ceos, and Hippias of Elis do. For each of them, my friends, can go into any city, and persuade the young men to leave the society of their fellow citizens, with any of whom they might associate for nothing, and to be only too glad to be allowed to pay money for the privilege of associating with themselves. And I believe that there is another wise man from Paros residing in Athens at this moment. I happened to meet Callias, the son of Hipponicus, a man who has spent more money on sophists than everyone else put together. So I said to him (he has two sons), "Callias, if your two sons had been foals or calves, we could have hired a trainer for them who would have trained them to excel in doing what they are naturally capable of. He would have been either a groom or a farmer. But whom do you intend to take to train them, seeing that they are men? Who understands the excellence which a man and citizen is capable of attaining? I suppose that you must have thought of this, because you have sons. Is there such a person or not?" "Certainly there is," he replied. "Who is he," said I, "and where does he come from, and what is his fee?" "Evenus, Socrates," he replied, "from Paros, five minae." Then I thought that Evenus was a fortunate person if he really understood this art and could teach so cleverly. If I had possessed knowledge of that kind, I should have been conceited and disdainful. But, Athenians, the truth is that I do not possess it.

Perhaps some of you may reply: "But, Socrates, what is the   V trouble with you? What has given rise to these prejudices against you? You must have been doing something out of the ordinary. All these rumors and reports of you would never have arisen if you had not been doing something different from other men. So tell us what it is, that we may not give our verdict arbitrarily." I think that that is a fair question, and I will try to explain to you what it is that has raised these prejudices against me and given me this reputation. Listen, then. Some of you, perhaps, will think that I am joking, but I assure you that I will tell you the whole truth. I have gained this reputation, Athenians, simply by reason of a certain wisdom. But by what kind of wisdom? It is by just that wisdom which is perhaps human wisdom. In that, it may be, I am really wise. But the men of whom I was speaking just now must be wise in a wisdom which is greater than human wisdom, or else I cannot describe it, for certainly I know nothing of it myself, and if any man says that I do, he lies and speaks to arouse prejudice against me. Do not interrupt me with shouts, Athenians, even if you think that I am boasting. What I am going to say is not my own statement. I will tell you who says it, and he is worthy of your respect. I will bring the god of Delphi to be the witness of my wisdom, if it is wisdom at all, and of its nature. You remember Chaerephon. From youth upwards he was my   21 comrade; and also a partisan of your democracy, sharing your recent exile [4] and returning with you. You remember, too, Chaerephon's character—how impulsive he was in carrying through whatever he took in hand. Once he went to Delphi and ventured to put this question to the oracle—I entreat you again, my friends, not to interrupt me with your shouts—he asked if there was anyone who was wiser than I. The priestess answered that there was no one. Chaerephon himself is dead, but his brother here will witness to what I say.

[4] During the totalitarian regime of The Thirty which remained in power for eight months (404 B.C.), five years before the trial.—Ed.

VI   Now see why I tell you this. I am going to explain to you
how the prejudice against me has arisen. When I heard of the
oracle I began to reflect: What can the god mean by this riddle?
I know very well that I am not wise, even in the smallest degree.
Then what can he mean by saying that I am the wisest of men?
It cannot be that he is speaking falsely, for he is a god and
cannot lie. For a long time I was at a loss to understand his
meaning. Then, very reluctantly, I turned to investigate it in
this manner: I went to a man who was reputed to be wise, thinking that there, if anywhere, I should prove the answer wrong, and
meaning to point out to the oracle its mistake, and to say, "You
said that I was the wisest of men, but this man is wiser than I
am." So I examined the man—I need not tell you his name, he
was a politician—but this was the result, Athenians. When I
conversed with him I came to see that, though a great many
persons, and most of all he himself, thought that he was wise,
yet he was not wise. Then I tried to prove to him that he was
not wise, though he fancied that he was. By so doing I made
him indignant, and many of the bystanders. So when I went
away, I thought to myself, "I am wiser than this man: neither
of us knows anything that is really worth knowing, but he
thinks that he has knowledge when he has not, while I, having
no knowledge, do not think that I have. I seem, at any rate, to
be a little wiser than he is on this point: I do not think that I
know what I do not know." Next I went to another man who
was reputed to be still wiser than the last, with exactly the same
result. And there again I made him, and many other men,
indignant.

VII   Then I went on to one man after another, realizing that I was
arousing indignation every day, which caused me much pain and
anxiety. Still I thought that I must set the god's command above
everything. So I had to go to every man who seemed to possess
any knowledge, and investigate the meaning of the oracle. Athe-
22   nians, I must tell you the truth; I swear, this was the result of
the investigation which I made at the god's command: I found
that the men whose reputation for wisdom stood highest were
nearly the most lacking in it, while others who were looked down

on as common people were much more intelligent. Now I must
describe to you the wanderings which I undertook, like Herculean
labors, to prove the oracle irrefutable. After the politicians, I
went to the poets, tragic, dithyrambic, and others, thinking that
there I should find myself manifestly more ignorant than they.
So I took up the poems on which I thought that they had spent
most pains, and asked them what they meant, hoping at the same
time to learn something from them. I am ashamed to tell you the
truth, my friends, but I must say it. Almost any one of the
bystanders could have talked about the works of these poets better
than the poets themselves. So I soon found that it is not by
wisdom that the poets create their works, but by a certain in-
stinctive inspiration, like soothsayers and prophets, who say
many fine things, but understand nothing of what they say.
The poets seemed to me to be in a similar situation. And at the
same time I perceived that, because of their poetry, they thought
that they were the wisest of men in other matters too, which
they were not. So I went away again, thinking that I had the same
advantage over the poets that I had over the politicians.

Finally, I went to the artisans, for I knew very well that I
possessed no knowledge at all worth speaking of, and I was sure
that I should find that they knew many fine things. And in that
I was not mistaken. They knew what I did not know, and so far
they were wiser than I. But, Athenians, it seemed to me that the
skilled artisans had the same failing as the poets. Each of them
believed himself to be extremely wise in matters of the greatest
importance because he was skillful in his own art: and this
presumption of theirs obscured their real wisdom. So I asked
myself, on behalf of the oracle, whether I would choose to remain
as I was, without either their wisdom or their ignorance, or to
possess both, as they did. And I answered to myself and to the
oracle that it was better for me to remain as I was.

From this examination, Athenians, has arisen much fierce
and bitter indignation, and as a result a great many prejudices
about me. People say that I am "a wise man." For the bystanders
always think that I am wise myself in any matter wherein I
refute another. But, gentlemen, I believe that the god is really

wise, and that by this oracle he meant that human wisdom is worth little or nothing. I do not think that he meant that Socrates was wise. He only made use of my name, and took me as an example, as though he would say to men, "He among you is the wisest who, like Socrates, knows that his wisdom is really worth nothing at all." Therefore I still go about testing and examining every man whom I think wise, whether he be a citizen or a stranger, as the god has commanded me. Whenever I find that he is not wise, I point out to him, on the god's behalf, that he is not wise. I am so busy in this pursuit that I have never had leisure to take any part worth mentioning in public matters or to look after my private affairs. I am in great poverty as the result of my service to the god.

X   Besides this, the young men who follow me about, who are the sons of wealthy persons and have the most leisure, take pleasure in hearing men cross-examined. They often imitate me among themselves; then they try their hands at cross-examining other people. And, I imagine, they find plenty of men who think that they know a great deal when in fact they know little or nothing. Then the persons who are cross-examined get angry with me instead of with themselves, and say that Socrates is an abomination and corrupts the young. When they are asked, "Why, what does he do? What does he teach?" they do not know what to say. Not to seem at a loss, they repeat the stock charges against all philosophers, and allege that he investigates things in the air and under the earth, and that he teaches people to disbelieve in the gods, and to make the worse argument appear the stronger. For, I suppose, they would not like to confess the truth, which is that they are shown up as ignorant pretenders to knowledge that they do not possess. So they have been filling your ears with their bitter prejudices for a long time, for they are ambitious, energetic, and numerous; and they speak vigorously and persuasively against me. Relying on this, Meletus, Anytus, and Lycon have attacked me. Meletus is indignant with me on behalf of the poets, Anytus on behalf of the artisans and politi-

24 cians, and Lycon on behalf of the orators. And so, as I said at the beginning, I shall be surprised if I am able, in the short

time allowed me for my defense, to remove from your minds this prejudice which has grown so strong. What I have told you, Athenians, is the truth: I neither conceal nor do I suppress anything, trivial or important. Yet I know that it is just this outspokenness which rouses indignation. But that is only a proof that my words are true, and that the prejudice against me, and the causes of it, are what I have said. And whether you investigate them now or hereafter, you will find that they are so.

What I have said must suffice as my defense against the **XI** charges of my first accusers. I will try next to defend myself against Meletus, that "good patriot," as he calls himself, and my later accusers. Let us assume that they are a new set of accusers, and read their indictment, as we did in the case of the others. It runs thus: Socrates is guilty of corrupting the youth, and of believing not in the gods whom the state believes in, but in other new divinities. Such is the accusation. Let us examine each point in it separately. Meletus says that I am guilty of corrupting the youth. But I say, Athenians, that he is guilty of playing a solemn joke by casually bringing men to trial, and pretending to have a solemn interest in matters to which he has never given a moment's thought. Now I will try to prove to you that this is so.

Come here, Meletus. Is it not a fact that you think it very **XII** important that the young should be as good as possible?

Meletus. It is.

Socrates. Come, then, tell the judges who improves them. You care so much,[5] you must know. You are accusing me, and bringing me to trial, because, as you say, you have discovered that I am the corrupter of the youth. Come now, reveal to the gentlemen who improves them. You see, Meletus, you have nothing to say; you are silent. But don't you think that this is shameful? Is not your silence a conclusive proof of what I say—that you have never cared? Come, tell us, my good man, who makes the young better?

Mel. The laws.

---

[5] Throughout the following passage Socrates plays on the etymology of the name "Meletus" as meaning "the man who cares."—Ed.

Socr. That, my friend, is not my question. What man improves the young, who begins by knowing the laws?

Mel. The judges here, Socrates.

Socr. What do you mean, Meletus? Can they educate the young and improve them?

Mel. Certainly.

Socr. All of them? Or only some of them?

Mel. All of them.

Socr. By Hera, that is good news! Such a large supply of
25 benefactors! And do the members of the audience here improve them, or not?

Mel. They do.

Socr. And do the councilors?

Mel. Yes.

Socr. Well, then, Meletus, do the members of the assembly corrupt the young or do they again all improve them?

Mel. They, too, improve them.

Socr. Then all the Athenians, apparently, make the young into good men except me, and I alone corrupt them. Is that your meaning?

Mel. Certainly, that is my meaning.

Socr. You have discovered me to be most unfortunate. Now tell me: do you think that the same holds good in the case of horses? Does one man do them harm and everyone else improve them? On the contrary, is it not one man only, or a very few—namely, those who are skilled with horses—who can improve them, while the majority of men harm them if they use them and have anything to do with them? Is it not so, Meletus, both with horses and with every other animal? Of course it is, whether you and Anytus say yes or no. The young would certainly be very fortunate if only one man corrupted them, and everyone else did them good. The truth is, Meletus, you prove conclusively that you have never thought about the young in your life. You exhibit your carelessness in not caring for the very matters about which you are prosecuting me.

XIII   Now be so good as to tell us, Meletus, is it better to live among good citizens or bad ones? Answer, my friend. I am not asking you at all a difficult question. Do not the bad harm their associates and the good do them good?

Mel. Yes.

Socr. Is there anyone who would rather be injured than benefited by his companions? Answer, my good man; you are obliged by the law to answer. Does anyone like to be injured?

Mel. Certainly not.

Socr. Well, then, are you prosecuting me for corrupting the young and making them worse, voluntarily or involuntarily?

Mel. For doing it voluntarily.

Socr. What, Meletus? Do you mean to say that you, who are so much younger than I, are yet so much wiser than I that you know that bad citizens always do evil, and that good citizens do good, to those with whom they come in contact, while I am so extraordinarily ignorant as not to know that, if I make any of my companions evil, he will probably injure me in some way? And you allege that I do this voluntarily? You will not make me believe that, nor anyone else either, I should think. Either I do not corrupt the young at all or, if I do, I do so involuntarily, so that you are lying in either case. And if I corrupt them involuntarily, the law does not call upon you to prosecute me for an error which is involuntary, but to take me aside privately and reprove and educate me. For, of course, I shall cease from doing wrong involuntarily, as soon as I know that I have been doing wrong. But you avoided associating with me and educating me; instead you bring me up before the court, where the law sends persons, not for education, but for punishment. 26

The truth is, Athenians, as I said, it is quite clear that Mele- XIV tus has never cared at all about these matters. However, now tell us, Meletus, how do you say that I corrupt the young? Clearly, according to your indictment, by teaching them not to believe in the gods the state believes in, but other new divinities instead. You mean that I corrupt the young by that teaching, do you not?

Mel. Yes, most certainly I mean that.

Socr. Then in the name of these gods of whom we are speaking, explain yourself a little more clearly to me and to these gentlemen here. I cannot understand what you mean. Do you mean that I teach the young to believe in some gods, but not in the gods of the state? Do you accuse me of teaching them to believe in strange gods? If that is your meaning, I myself believe in some gods, and my crime is not that of complete atheism. Or do you mean that I do not believe in the gods at all myself, and that I teach other people not to believe in them either?

Mel. I mean that you do not believe in the gods in any way whatever.

Socr. You amaze me, Meletus! Why do you say that? Do you mean that I believe neither the sun nor the moon to be gods, like other men?

Mel. I swear he does not, judges. He says that the sun is a stone, and the moon earth.

Socr. My dear Meletus, do you think that you are prosecuting Anaxagoras? You must have a very poor opinion of these men, and think them illiterate, if you imagine that they do not know that the works of Anaxagoras of Clazomenae are full of these doctrines. And so young men learn these things from me, when they can often buy them in the theater for a drachma at most, and laugh at Socrates were he to pretend that these doctrines, which are very peculiar doctrines, too, were his own. But please tell me, do you really think that I do not believe in the gods at all?

Mel. Most certainly I do. You are a complete atheist.

Socr. No one believes that, Meletus, not even you yourself. It seems to me, Athenians, that Meletus is very insolent and reckless, and that he is prosecuting me simply out of insolence, recklessness, and youthful bravado. For he seems to be testing me, 27 by asking me a riddle that has no answer. "Will this wise Socrates," he says to himself, "see that I am joking and contradicting myself? Or shall I deceive him and everyone else who hears me?" Meletus seems to me to contradict himself in his indictment: it is as if he were to say, "Socrates is guilty of not believing in the gods, but believes in the gods." This is joking.

XV   Now, my friends, let us see why I think that this is his meaning. You must answer me, Meletus, and you, Athenians, must remember the request which I made to you at the start, and not interrupt me with shouts if I talk in my usual manner.

Is there any man, Meletus, who believes in the existence of things pertaining to men and not in the existence of men? Make him answer the question, gentlemen, without these interruptions. Is there any man who believes in the existence of horsemanship and not in the existence of horses? Or in flute playing and not in flute players? There is not, my friend. If you will not answer, I will tell both you and the judges. But you must answer my next question. Is there any man who believes in the existence of divine things and not in the existence of divinities?

Mel. There is not.

Socr. I am very glad that these gentlemen have managed to extract an answer from you. Well then, you say that I believe in divine things, whether they be old or new, and that I teach others to believe in them. At any rate, according to your statement, I believe in divine things. That you have sworn in your indictment. But if I believe in divine things, I suppose it follows necessarily that I believe in divinities. Is it not so? It is. I assume that you grant that, as you do not answer. But do we not believe that divinities are either gods themselves or the children of the gods? Do you admit that?

Mel. I do.

Socr. Then you admit that I believe in divinities. Now, if these divinities are gods, then, as I say, you are joking and asking a riddle, and asserting that I do not believe in the gods, and at the same time that I do, since I believe in divinities. But if these divinities are the illegitimate children of the gods, either by the nymphs or by other mothers, as they are said to be, then, I ask, what man could believe in the existence of the children of the gods, and not in the existence of the gods? That would be as absurd as believing in the existence of the offspring of horses and asses, and not in the existence of horses and asses. You must have indicted me in this manner, Meletus, either to test me or because you could not find any act of injustice that you could accuse me of with truth. But you will never contrive to persuade any man with any sense at all that a belief in divine things and

28   things of the gods does not necessarily involve a belief in divinities, and in the gods.

XVI   But in truth, Athenians, I do not think that I need say very much to prove that I have not committed the act of injustice for which Meletus is prosecuting me. What I have said is enough to prove that. But be assured it is certainly true, as I have already told you, that I have aroused much indignation. That is what will cause my condemnation if I am condemned; not Meletus nor Anytus either, but that prejudice and resentment of the multitude which have been the destruction of many good men before me, and I think will be so again. There is no prospect that I shall be the last victim.

Perhaps someone will say: "Are you not ashamed, Socrates, of leading a life which is very likely now to cause your death?" I should answer him with justice, and say: "My friend, if you think that a man of any worth at all ought to reckon the chances of life and death when he acts, or that he ought to think of anything but whether he is acting justly or unjustly, and as a good or a bad man would act, you are mistaken. According to you, the demigods who died at Troy would be foolish, and among them Achilles, who thought nothing of danger when the alternative was disgrace. For when his mother—and she was a goddess—addressed him, when he was resolved to slay Hector, in this fashion, 'My son, if you avenge the death of your comrade Patroclus and slay Hector, you will die yourself, for fate awaits you next after Hector.' When he heard this, he scorned danger and death; he feared much more to live a coward and not to avenge his friend. 'Let me punish the evildoer and afterwards die,' he said, 'that I may not remain here by the beaked ships jeered at, encumbering the earth.' " [6] Do you suppose that he thought of danger or of death? For this, Athenians, I believe to be the truth. Wherever a man's station is, whether he has chosen it of his own will, or whether he has been placed at it by his commander, there it is his duty to remain and face the danger without thinking of death or of any other thing except disgrace.

[6] Homer, *Iliad*, xviii, 96, 98.—Ed.

When the generals whom you chose to command me, Athe-   XVII
nians, assigned me my station during the battles of Potidaea,
Amphipolis, and Delium, I remained where they stationed me and
ran the risk of death, like other men. It would be very strange con-
duct on my part if I were to desert my station now from fear of
death or of any other thing when the god has commanded me—as I
am persuaded that he has done—to spend my life in searching for   29
wisdom, and in examining myself and others. That would indeed
be a very strange thing. Then certainly I might with justice be
brought to trial for not believing in the gods, for I should be
disobeying the oracle, and fearing death and thinking myself wise
when I was not wise. For to fear death, my friends, is only to
think ourselves wise without really being wise, for it is to think
that we know what we do not know. For no one knows whether
death may not be the greatest good that can happen to man. But
men fear it as if they knew quite well that it was the greatest of
evils. And what is this but that shameful ignorance of thinking
that we know what we do not know? In this matter, too, my
friends, perhaps I am different from the multitude. And if I were
to claim to be at all wiser than others, it would be because, not
knowing very much about the other world, I do not think I
know. But I do know very well that it is evil and disgraceful to
do an unjust act, and to disobey my superior, whether man or
god. I will never do what I know to be evil, and shrink in fear
from what I do not know to be good or evil. Even if you acquit
me now, and do not listen to Anytus' argument that, if I am to
be acquitted, I ought never to have been brought to trial at all,
and that, as it is, you are bound to put me to death because, as
he said, if I escape, all your sons will be utterly corrupted by
practicing what Socrates teaches. If you were therefore to say
to me, "Socrates, this time we will not listen to Anytus. We will
let you go, but on the condition that you give up this investigation of yours, and philosophy. If you are found following these
pursuits again, you shall die." I say, if you offered to let me go
on these terms, I should reply: "Athenians, I hold you in the
highest regard and affection, but I will be persuaded by the god
rather than you. As long as I have breath and strength I

will not give up philosophy and exhorting you and declaring the truth to every one of you whom I meet, saying, as I am accustomed, 'My good friend, you are a citizen of Athens, a city which is very great and very famous for its wisdom and power—are you not ashamed of caring so much for the making of money and for fame and prestige, when you neither think nor care about wisdom and truth and the improvement of your soul?' " If he disputes my words and says that he does care about these things, I shall not at once release him and go away: I shall question him and cross-examine him and test him. If I think that he has not attained excellence, though he says that he

30 has, I shall reproach him for undervaluing the most valuable things, and overvaluing those that are less valuable. This I shall do to everyone whom I meet, young or old, citizen or stranger, but especially to citizens, since they are more closely related to me. This, you must recognize, the god has commanded me to do. And I think that no greater good has ever befallen you in the state than my service to the god. For I spend my whole life in going about and persuading you all to give your first and greatest care to the improvement of your souls, and not till you have done that to think of your bodies or your wealth. And I tell you that wealth does not bring excellence, but that wealth, and every other good thing which men have, whether in public or in private, comes from excellence. If then I corrupt the youth by this teaching, these things must be harmful. But if any man says that I teach anything else, there is nothing in what he says. And therefore, Athenians, I say, whether you are persuaded by Anytus or not, whether you acquit me or not, I shall not change my way of life; no, not if I have to die for it many times.

XVIII   Do not interrupt me, Athenians, with your shouts. Remember the request which I made to you, and do not interrupt my words. I think that it will profit you to hear them. I am going to say something more to you, at which you may be inclined to protest, but do not do that. Be sure that if you put me to death, I who am what I have told you that I am, you will do yourselves more harm than me. Meletus and Anytus can do me no harm: that is impossible, for I am sure it is not allowed that a good man be injured by a worse. He may indeed kill me, or drive me into exile, or deprive me of my civil rights. Perhaps Meletus and others think those things great evils. But I do not think so. I think it is a much greater evil to do what he is doing now, and to try to put a man to death unjustly. And now, Athenians, I am not arguing in my own defense at all, as you might expect me to do, but rather in yours in order you may not make a mistake about the gift of the god to you by condemning me. For if you put me to death, you will not easily find another who, if I may use a ludicrous comparison, clings to the state as a sort of gadfly to a horse that is large and well-bred but rather sluggish because of its size, so that it needs to be aroused. It seems to me that the god has attached me like that to the state, for I am constantly alighting upon you at every point to arouse, persuade, and reproach each of 31 you all day long. You will not easily find anyone else, my friends, to fill my place; and if you are persuaded by me, you will spare my life. You are indignant, as drowsy persons are when they are awakened, and, of course, if you are persuaded by Anytus, you could easily kill me with a single blow, and then sleep on undisturbed for the rest of your lives, unless the god in his care for you sends another to arouse you. And you may easily see that it is the god who has given me to your city; for it is not human, the way in which I have neglected all my own interests and allowed my private affairs to be neglected for so many years, while occupying myself unceasingly in your interests, going to each of you privately, like a father or an elder brother, trying to persuade him to care for human excellence. There would have been a reason for it, if I had gained any advantage by this, or if I had been paid for my exhortations; but you see yourselves that my accusers, though they accuse me of everything else without shame, have not had the shamelessness to say that I ever either exacted or demanded payment. To that they have no witness. And I think that I have sufficient witness to the truth of what I say—my poverty.

Perhaps it may seem strange to you that, though I go about XIX giving this advice privately and meddling in others' affairs, yet I do not venture to come forward in the assembly and advise the state. You have often heard me speak of my reason for this, and in many places: it is that I have a certain divine guide, which is what Meletus has caricatured in his indictment. I have had it from childhood. It is a kind of voice which, whenever I hear it, always turns me back from something which I was going to do, but never urges me to act. It is this which forbids me to take part in politics. And I think it does well to forbid me. For, Athenians, it is quite certain that, if I had attempted to take part in politics, I should have perished at once and long ago without doing any good either to you or to myself. And do not be indignant with me for telling the truth. There is no man who will preserve his life for long, either in Athens or elsewhere, if he firmly opposes the multitude, and tries to prevent the commission of much injustice and illegality in the state. He who 32 would really fight for justice must do so as a private citizen, not as a political figure, if he is to preserve his life, even for a short time.

XX   I will prove to you that this is so by very strong evidence, not by mere words, but by what you value more—actions. Listen, then, to what has happened to me, that you may know that there is no man who could make me consent to commit an unjust act from the fear of death, but that I would perish at once rather than give way. What I am going to tell you may be commonplace in the law court; nevertheless, it is true. The only office that I ever held in the state, Athenians, was that of councilor. When you wished to try the ten admirals who did not rescue their men after the battle of Arginusae as a group, which was illegal, as you all came to think afterwards, the executive committee was composed of members of the tribe Antiochis, to which I belong.[7] On that occasion I alone of the committee members opposed your illegal action and gave my vote against you. The orators were ready to impeach me and arrest me; and you were

[7] The Council was the administrative body in Athens. Actual administrative functions were performed by an executive committee of the Council, and the members of this committee were recruited from each tribe in turn. The case Socrates is alluding to was that of the admirals who were accused of having failed to rescue the crews of ships which sank during the battle of Arginusae. The six admirals who were actually put on trial were condemned as a group and executed.—Ed.

clamoring and urging them on with your shouts. But I thought that I ought to face the danger, with law and justice on my side, rather than join with you in your unjust proposal, from fear of imprisonment or death. That was when the state was democratic. When the oligarchy came in, The Thirty sent for me, with four others, to the council-chamber, and ordered us to bring Leon the Salaminian from Salamis, that they might put him to death. They were in the habit of frequently giving similar orders to many others, wishing to implicate as many as possible in their crimes. But then I again proved, not by mere words, but by my actions, that, if I may speak bluntly, I do not care a straw for death; but that I do care very much indeed about not doing anything unjust or impious. That government with all its power did not terrify me into doing anything unjust. When we left the council-chamber, the other four went over to Salamis and brought Leon across to Athens; I went home. And if the rule of The Thirty had not been overthrown soon afterwards, I should very likely have been put to death for what I did then. Many of you will be my witnesses in this matter.[8]

Now do you think that I could have remained alive all these years if I had taken part in public affairs, and had always maintained the cause of justice like a good man, and had held it a paramount duty, as it is, to do so? Certainly not, Athenians, nor could any other man. But throughout my whole life, both in private and in public, whenever I have had to take part in public affairs, you will find I have always been the same and have never yielded unjustly to anyone; no, not to those whom my enemies falsely assert to have been my pupils. But I was never anyone's teacher. I have never withheld myself from anyone, young or old,

XXI

33

[8] There is evidence that Meletus was one of the four who turned in Leon. Socrates' recalling this earlier lapse from legal procedure is probably also a thrust at Anytus. The Thirty successfully implicated so many Athenians in their crimes that an amnesty was declared, which Anytus strongly favored, in order to enlist wider support for the restored democracy. Thus those who were really implicated could now no longer be prosecuted legally, but Socrates is himself being illegally prosecuted (as he now goes on to suggest) because he was guilty of having associated with such "pupils" as Critias, who was a leader of The Thirty.—Ed.

who was anxious to hear me converse while I was making my investigation; neither do I converse for payment, and refuse to converse without payment. I am ready to ask questions of rich and poor alike, and if any man wishes to answer me, and then listen to what I have to say, he may. And I cannot justly be charged with causing these men to turn out good or bad, for I never either taught or professed to teach any of them any knowledge whatever. And if any man asserts that he ever learned or heard anything from me in private which everyone else did not hear as well as he, be sure that he does not speak the truth.

XXII   Why is it, then, that people delight in spending so much time in my company? You have heard why, Athenians. I told you the whole truth when I said that they delight in hearing me examine persons who think that they are wise when they are not wise. It is certainly very amusing to listen to. And, as I have said, the god has commanded me to examine men, in oracles and in dreams and in every way in which the divine will was ever declared to man. This is the truth, Athenians, and if it were not the truth, it would be easily refuted. For if it were really the case that I have already corrupted some of the young men, and am now corrupting others, surely some of them, finding as they grew older that I had given them bad advice in their youth, would have come forward today to accuse me and take their revenge. Or if they were unwilling to do so themselves, surely their relatives, their fathers or brothers, or others, would, if I had done them any harm, have remembered it and taken their revenge. Certainly I see many of them in court. Here is Crito, of my own district and of my own age, the father of Critobulus; here is Lysanias of Sphettus, the father of Aeschines; here is also Antiphon of Cephisus, the father of Epigenes. Then here are others whose brothers have spent their time in my company—Nicostratus, the son of Theozotides and brother of Theodotus—and Theodotus is dead, so he at least cannot entreat his brother to be silent; here is Paralus, the son of Demodocus and the brother of Theages; here is Adeimantus, the son of Ariston, whose brother is Plato here; and Aeantodorus, whose brother is Aristodorus. And I can name many others to you, some of whom Meletus ought to have called as witnesses in the course of his own speech; but if he forgot to call them then, let him call them now—I will yield the floor to him—and tell us if he has any such evidence. No, on the contrary, my friends, you will find all these men ready to support me, the corrupter who has injured their relatives, as Meletus and Anytus call me. Those of them who have been already corrupted might perhaps have some reason for supporting me, but what reason can their relatives have who are grown up, and who are uncorrupted, except the reason of truth and justice— that they know very well that Meletus is lying, and that I am speaking the truth?

Well, my friends, this, and perhaps more like this, is pretty much all I have to offer in my defense. There may be some one among you who will be indignant when he remembers how, even in a less important trial than this, he begged and entreated the judges, with many tears, to acquit him, and brought forward his children and many of his friends and relatives in court in order to appeal to your feelings; and then finds that I shall do none of these things, though I am in what he would think the supreme danger. Perhaps he will harden himself against me when he notices this; it may make him angry, and he may cast his vote in anger. If it is so with any of you—I do not suppose that it is, but in case it should be so—I think that I should answer him reasonably if I said: "My friend, I have relatives, too, for, in the words of Homer, I am 'not born of an oak or a rock' [9] but of flesh and blood." And so, Athenians, I have relatives, and I have three sons, one of them nearly grown up, and the other two still children. Yet I will not bring any of them forward before you and implore you to acquit me. And why will I do none of these things? It is not from arrogance, Athenians, nor because I lack respect for you— whether or not I can face death bravely is another question— but for my own good name, and for your good name, and for the good name of the whole state. I do not think it right, at my age and with my reputation, to do anything of that kind. Rightly or wrongly, men have made up their minds that in some way Socrates is different from the multitude of men. And it will be

[9] Homer, *Odyssey*, xix, 163.

XXIII

35

shameful if those of you who are thought to excel in wisdom, or in bravery, or in any other excellence, are going to act in this fashion. I have often seen men of reputation behaving in an extraordinary way at their trial, as if they thought it a terrible fate to be killed, and as though they expected to live for ever if you did not put them to death. Such men seem to me to bring shame upon the state, for any stranger would suppose that the best and most eminent Athenians, who are selected by their fellow citizens to hold office, and for other honors, are no better than women. Those of you, Athenians, who have any reputation at all ought not to do these things, and you ought not to allow us to do them. You should show that you will be much more ready to condemn men who make the state ridiculous by these pathetic performances than men who remain quiet.

XXIV   But apart from the question of reputation, my friends, I do not think that it is right to entreat the judge to acquit us, or to escape condemnation in that way. It is our duty to teach and persuade him. He does not sit to give away justice as a favor, but to pronounce judgment; and he has sworn, not to favor any man whom he would like to favor, but to judge according to law. And, therefore, we ought not to encourage you in the habit of breaking your oaths; and you ought not to allow yourselves to fall into this habit, for then neither you nor we would be acting piously. Therefore, Athenians, do not require me to do these things, for I believe them to be neither good nor just nor pious; especially, do not ask me to do them today when Meletus is prosecuting me for impiety. For were I to be successful and persuade you by my entreaties to break your oaths, I should be clearly teaching you to believe that there are no gods, and I should be simply accusing myself by my defense of not believing in them. But, Athenians, that is very far from the truth. I do believe in the gods as no one of my accusers believes in them; and to you and to the god I commit my cause to be decided as is best for you and for me.

(He is found guilty by 281 votes to 220.)

XXV   I am not indignant at the verdict which you have given,
36   Athenians, for many reasons. I expected that you would find

me guilty; and I am not so much surprised at that as at the numbers of the votes. I certainly never thought that the majority against me would have been so narrow. But now it seems that if only thirty votes had changed sides, I should have escaped. So I think that I have escaped Meletus, as it is; and not only have I escaped him, for it is perfectly clear that if Anytus and Lycon had not come forward to accuse me, too, he would not have obtained the fifth part of the votes, and would have had to pay a fine of a thousand drachmae.

So he proposes death as the penalty. Be it so. And what **XXVI** alternative penalty shall I propose to you, Athenians? [10] What I deserve, of course, must I not? What then do I deserve to pay or to suffer for having determined not to spend my life in ease? I neglected the things which most men value, such as wealth, and family interests, and military commands, and public oratory, and all the civic appointments, and social clubs, and political factions, that there are in Athens; for I thought that I was really too honest a man to preserve my life if I engaged in these affairs. So I did not go where I should have done no good either to you or to myself. I went, instead, to each one of you privately to do him, as I say, the greatest of benefits, and tried to persuade him not to think of his affairs until he had thought of himself and tried to make himself as good and wise as possible, nor to think of the affairs of Athens until he had thought of Athens herself; and to care for other things in the same manner. Then what do I deserve for such a life? Something good, Athenians, if I am really to propose what I deserve; and something good which it would be suitable for me to receive. Then what is a suitable reward to be given to a poor benefactor who requires leisure to exhort you? There is no reward, Athenians, so suitable for him as receiving free meals in the prytaneum. It is a much more suitable reward for him than for any of you who has won a victory at the Olympic games with his horse or his chariots. Such a man only

---

[10] For certain crimes no penalty was fixed by Athenian law. Having reached a verdict of guilty, the court had still to decide between the alternative penalties proposed by the prosecution and the defense.—Ed.

makes you seem happy, but I make you really happy; he is not in want, and I am. So if I am to propose the penalty which I really deserve, I propose this—free meals in the prytaneum.

37
XXVII Perhaps you think me stubborn and arrogant in what I am saying now, as in what I said about the entreaties and tears. It is not so, Athenians. It is rather that I am convinced that I never wronged any man voluntarily, though I cannot persuade you of that, since we have conversed together only a little time. If there were a law at Athens, as there is elsewhere, not to finish a trial of life and death in a single day, I think that I could have persuaded you; but now it is not easy in so short a time to clear myself of great prejudices. But when I am persuaded that I have never wronged any man, I shall certainly not wrong myself, or admit that I deserve to suffer any evil, or propose any evil for myself as a penalty. Why should I? Lest I should suffer the penalty which Meletus proposes when I say that I do not know whether it is a good or an evil? Shall I choose instead of it something which I know to be an evil, and propose that as a penalty? Shall I propose imprisonment? And why should I pass the rest of my days in prison, the slave of successive officials? Or shall I propose a fine, with imprisonment until it is paid? I have told you why I will not do that. I should have to remain in prison, for I have no money to pay a fine with. Shall I then propose exile? Perhaps you would agree to that. Life would indeed be very dear to me if I were unreasonable enough to expect that strangers would cheerfully tolerate my discussions and arguments when you who are my fellow citizens cannot endure them, and have found them so irksome and odious to you that you are seeking now to be relieved of them. No, indeed, Athenians, that is not likely. A fine life I should lead for an old man if I were to withdraw from Athens and pass the rest of my days in wandering from city to city, and continually being expelled. For I know very well that the young men will listen to me wherever I go, as they do here. If I drive them away, they will persuade their elders to expel me; if I do not drive them away, their fathers and other relatives will expel me for their sakes.

Perhaps someone will say, "Why cannot you withdraw from XXVIII
Athens, Socrates, and hold your peace?" It is the most difficult
thing in the world to make you understand why I cannot do that.
If I say that I cannot hold my peace because that would be to
disobey the god, you will think that I am not in earnest and will
not believe me. And if I tell you that no greater good can happen 38
to a man than to discuss human excellence every day and the
other matters about which you have heard me arguing and examining myself and others, and that an unexamined life is not
worth living, then you will believe me still less. But that is so, my
friends, though it is not easy to persuade you. And, what is more,
I am not accustomed to think that I deserve anything evil. If I
had been rich, I would have proposed as large a fine as I could
pay: that would have done me no harm. But I am not rich enough
to pay a fine unless you are willing to fix it at a sum within my
means. Perhaps I could pay you a mina, so I propose that. Plato
here, Athenians, and Crito, and Critobulus, and Apollodorus bid
me propose thirty minae, and they guarantee its payment. So
I propose thirty minae. Their security will be sufficient to you
for the money.

(*He is condemned to death.*)

You have not gained very much time, Athenians, and at XXIX
the price of the slurs of those who wish to revile the state. And
they will say that you put Socrates, a wise man, to death. For
they will certainly call me wise, whether I am wise or not, when
they want to reproach you. If you had waited for a little
while, your wishes would have been fulfilled in the course
of nature; for you see that I am an old man, far advanced
in years, and near to death. I am saying this not to all of you,
only to those who have voted for my death. And to them I have
something else to say. Perhaps, my friends, you think that I
have been convicted because I was wanting in the arguments by
which I could have persuaded you to acquit me, if I had thought
it right to do or to say anything to escape punishment. It is
not so. I have been convicted because I was wanting, not in

arguments, but in impudence and shamelessness—because I
would not plead before you as you would have liked to hear me
plead, or appeal to you with weeping and wailing, or say and do
many other things which I maintain are unworthy of me, but
which you have been accustomed to from other men. But when
I was defending myself, I thought that I ought not to do anything
unworthy of a free man because of the danger which I ran, and
I have not changed my mind now. I would very much rather
defend myself as I did, and die, than as you would have had me
do, and live. Both in a lawsuit and in war, there are some things

39 which neither I nor any other man may do in order to escape
from death. In battle, a man often sees that he may at least
escape from death by throwing down his arms and falling on his
knees before the pursuer to beg for his life. And there are many
other ways of avoiding death in every danger if a man is willing
to say and to do anything. But, my friends, I think that it is a
much harder thing to escape from wickedness than from death,
for wickedness is swifter than death. And now I, who am old and
slow, have been overtaken by the slower pursuer: and my accusers, who are clever and swift, have been overtaken by the swifter
pursuer—wickedness. And now I shall go away, sentenced by you
to death; they will go away, sentenced by truth to wickedness
and injustice. And I abide by this award as well as they. Perhaps
it was right for these things to be so. I think that they are
fairly balanced.

XXX   And now I wish to prophesy to you, Athenians, who have
condemned me. For I am going to die, and that is the time when
men have most prophetic power. And I prophesy to you who have
sentenced me to death that a far more severe punishment than
you have inflicted on me will surely overtake you as soon as I
am dead. You have done this thing, thinking that you will be
relieved from having to give an account of your lives. But I say
that the result will be very different. There will be more men
who will call you to account, whom I have held back, though
you did not recognize it. And they will be harsher toward you
than I have been, for they will be younger, and you will be more
indignant with them. For if you think that you will restrain men

from reproaching you for not living as you should, by putting them to death, you are very much mistaken. That way of escape is neither possible nor honorable. It is much more honorable and much easier not to suppress others, but to make yourselves as good as you can. This is my parting prophecy to you who have condemned me.

With you who have acquitted me I should like to discuss   XXXI
this thing that has happened, while the authorities are busy, and before I go to the place where I have to die. So, remain with me until I go: there is no reason why we should not talk with each other while it is possible. I wish to explain to you, as my friends,   40
the meaning of what has happened to me. An amazing thing has happened to me, judges—for I am right in calling you judges.[11] The prophetic guide has been constantly with me all through my life till now, opposing me even in trivial matters if I were not going to act rightly. And now you yourselves see what has happened to me—a thing which might be thought, and which is sometimes actually reckoned, the supreme evil. But the divine guide did not oppose me when I was leaving my house in the morning, nor when I was coming up here to the court, nor at any point in my speech when I was going to say anything; though at other times it has often stopped me in the very act of speaking. But now, in this matter, it has never once opposed me, either in my words or my actions. I will tell you what I believe to be the reason. This thing that has come upon me must be a good; and those of us who think that death is an evil must needs be mistaken. I have a clear proof that that is so; for my accustomed guide would certainly have opposed me if I had not been going to meet with something good.

And if we reflect in another way, we shall see that we may   XXXII
well hope that death is a good. For the state of death is one of two things: either the dead man wholly ceases to be and loses all consciousness or, as we are told, it is a change and a migration of the soul to another place. And if death is the absence of all

[11] The form of address hitherto has always been "Athenians," or "my friends." The "judges" in an Athenian court were simply the members of the jury.—Ed.

consciousness, and like the sleep of one whose slumbers are unbroken by any dreams, it will be a wonderful gain. For if a man had to select that night in which he slept so soundly that he did not even dream, and had to compare with it all the other nights and days of his life, and then had to say how many days and nights in his life he had spent better and more pleasantly than this night, I think that a private person, nay, even the Great King of Persia himself, would find them easy to count, compared with the others. If that is the nature of death, I for one count it a gain. For then it appears that all time is nothing more than a single night. But if death is a journey to another place, and what we are told is true—that all who have died are there—what good could be greater than this, my judges? Would a journey not be worth taking, at the end of which, in the other world, we should be delivered from the pretended judges here and should find the true judges who are said to sit in judgment below, such as Minos and Rhadamanthus and Aeacus and Triptolemus, and the other demigods who were just in their own lives? Or what would you not give to converse with Orpheus and Musaeus and Hesiod and Homer? I am willing to die many times if this be true. And for my own part I should find it wonderful to meet there Palamedes, and Ajax the son of Telamon, and the other men of old who have died through an unjust judgment, and to compare my experiences with theirs. That I think would be no small pleasure. And, above all, I could spend my time in examining those who are there, as I examine men here, and in finding out which of them is wise, and which of them thinks himself wise when he is not wise. What would we not give, my judges, to be able to examine the leader of the great expedition against Troy, or Odysseus, or Sisyphus, or countless other men and women whom we could name? It would be an inexpressible happiness to converse with them and to live with them and to examine them. Assuredly there they do not put men to death for doing that. For besides the other ways in which they are happier than we are, they are immortal, at least if what we are told is true.

LXXIII And you too, judges, must face death hopefully, and believe this one truth, that no evil can happen to a good man, either in life or after death. His affairs are not neglected by the gods; and what has happened to me today has not happened by chance. I am persuaded that it was better for me to die now, and to be released from trouble; and that was the reason why the guide never turned me back. And so I am not at all angry with my accusers or with those who have condemned me to die. Yet it was not with this in mind that they accused me and condemned me, but meaning to do me an injury. So far I may blame them.

Yet I have one request to make of them. When my sons grow up, punish them, my friends, and harass them in the same way that I have harassed you, if they seem to you to care for riches or for any other thing more than excellence; and if they think that they are something when they are really nothing, reproach them, as I have reproached you, for not caring for what they should, and for thinking that they are something when really they are nothing. And if you will do this, I myself and my sons will have 42 received justice from you.

But now the time has come, and we must go away—I to die, and you to live. Which is better is known to the god alone.

CRITO

Socrates. Why have you come at this hour, Crito? Is it not still early?

St. I
p. 43

Crito. Yes, very early.

Socr. About what time is it?

Crito. It is just daybreak.

Socr. I wonder that the jailer was willing to let you in.

Crito. He knows me now, Socrates; I come here so often, and besides, I have given him a tip.

Socr. Have you been here long?

Crito. Yes, some time.

Socr. Then why did you sit down without speaking? Why did you not wake me at once?

Crito. Indeed, Socrates, I wish that I myself were not so sleepless and sorrowful. But I have been wondering to see how soundly you sleep. And I purposely did not wake you, for I was anxious not to disturb your repose. Often before, all through your life, I have thought that your temperament was a happy one; and I think so more than ever now when I see how easily and calmly you bear the calamity that has come to you.

Socr. Nay, Crito, it would be absurd if at my age I were disturbed at having to die.

Crito. Other men as old are overtaken by similar calamities, Socrates; but their age does not save them from being disturbed by their fate.

51

Socr. That is so; but tell me why are you here so early?

Crito. I am the bearer of sad news, Socrates; not sad, it seems, for you, but for me and for all your friends, both sad and hard to bear; and for none of them, I think, is it as hard to bear as it is for me.

Socr. What is it? Has the ship come from Delos, at the arrival of which I am to die?

Crito. No, it has not actually arrived, but I think that it will be here today, from the news which certain persons have brought from Sunium, who left it there. It is clear from their report that it will be here today; and so, Socrates, tomorrow your life will have to end.

II
44

Socr. Well, Crito, may it end well. Be it so, if so the gods will. But I do not think that the ship will be here today.

Crito. Why do you suppose not?

Socr. I will tell you. I am to die on the day after the ship arrives, am I not? [1]

Crito. That is what the authorities say.

Socr. Then I do not think that it will come today, but tomorrow. I am counting on a dream I had a little while ago in the night, so it seems to be fortunate that you did not wake me.

Crito. And what was this dream?

Socr. A fair and beautiful woman, clad in white, seemed to come to me, and call me and say, "O Socrates—

On the third day shall you fertile Phthia reach." [2]

Crito. What a strange dream, Socrates!

Socr. But its meaning is clear, at least to me, Crito.

III

Crito. Yes, too clear, it seems. But, O my good Socrates, I beg you for the last time to listen to me and save yourself. For to me your death will be more than a single disaster; not only shall I lose a friend the like of whom I shall never find again, but many persons who do not know you and me well will think

---

[1] Criminals could not be put to death while the sacred ship was away on its voyage.—Ed.

[2] Homer, *Iliad*, ix, 363.

that I might have saved you if I had been willing to spend money, but that I neglected to do so. And what reputation could be more disgraceful than the reputation of caring more for money than for one's friends? The public will never believe that we were anxious to save you, but that you yourself refused to escape.

Socr. But, my dear Crito, why should we care so much about public opinion? Reasonable men, of whose opinion it is worth our while to think, will believe that we acted as we really did.

Crito. But you see, Socrates, that it is necessary to care about public opinion, too. This very thing that has happened to you proves that the multitude can do a man not the least, but almost the greatest harm, if he is falsely accused to them.

Socr. I wish that the multitude were able to do a man the greatest harm, Crito, for then they would be able to do him the greatest good, too. That would have been fine. But, as it is, they can do neither. They cannot make a man either wise or foolish: they act wholly at random.

Crito. Well, as you wish. But tell me this, Socrates. You IV surely are not anxious about me and your other friends, and afraid lest, if you escape, the informers would say that we stole you away, and get us into trouble, and involve us in a great deal of expense, or perhaps in the loss of all our property, and, it may be, bring some other punishment upon us besides? If you have any fear of that kind, dismiss it. For of course we are bound to 45 run these risks, and still greater risks than these, if necessary, in saving you. So do not, I beg you, refuse to listen to me.

Socr. I am anxious about that, Crito, and about much besides.

Crito. Then have no fear on that score. There are men who, for no very large sum, are ready to bring you out of prison into safety. And then, you know, these informers are cheaply bought, and there would be no need to spend much upon them. My fortune is at your service, and I think that it is adequate; and if you have any feeling about making use of my money, there are strangers in Athens whom you know, ready to use theirs; and one of them, Simmias of Thebes, has actually brought enough for this very purpose. And Cebes and many others are ready, too. And therefore, I repeat, do not shrink from saving yourself on that ground. And do not let what you said in the court—that if you went into exile you would not know what to do with yourself—stand in your way; for there are many places for you to go to, where you will be welcomed. If you choose to go to Thessaly, I have friends there who will make much of you and protect you from any annoyance from the people of Thessaly.

V   And besides, Socrates, I think that you will be doing what is unjust if you abandon your life when you might preserve it. You are simply playing into your enemies' hands; it is exactly what they wanted—to destroy you. And what is more, to me you seem to be abandoning your children, too. You will leave them to take their chance in life, as far as you are concerned, when you might bring them up and educate them. Most likely their fate will be the usual fate of children who are left orphans. But you ought not to bring children into the world unless you mean to take the trouble of bringing them up and educating them. It seems to me that you are choosing the easy way, and not the way of a good and brave man, as you ought, when you have been talking all your life long of the value that you set upon human excellence. For my part, I feel ashamed both for you and for us who are your friends. Men will think that the whole thing which has happened to you—your appearance in court to face trial, when you need not have appeared at all; the very way in which the trial was conducted; and then last of all this, the crowning absurdity of the whole affair—is due to our cowardice. It will look as if we had shirked the danger out of miserable
46 cowardice; for we did not save you, and you did not save yourself, when it was quite possible to do so if we had been good for anything at all. Take care, Socrates, lest these things be not evil only, but also dishonorable to you and to us. Reflect, then, or rather the time for reflection is past; we must make up our minds. And there is only one plan possible. Everything must be done tonight. If we delay any longer, we are lost. Socrates, I implore you not to refuse to listen to me.

VI   *Socr.* My dear Crito, if your anxiety to save me be right, it is most valuable; but if not, the greater it is the harder it will be to cope with. We must reflect, then, whether we are to do as you say or not; for I am still what I always have been —a man who will accept no argument but that which on reflection I find to be truest. I cannot cast aside my former arguments because this misfortune has come to me. They seem to me to be as true as ever they were, and I respect and honor the same ones as I used to. And if we have no better argument to substitute for them, I certainly shall not agree to your proposal, not even though the power of the multitude should scare us with fresh terrors, as children are scared with hobgoblins, and inflict upon us new fines and imprisonments, and deaths. What is the most appropriate way of examining the question? Shall we go back first to what you say about opinions, and ask if we used to be right in thinking that we ought to pay attention to some opinions, and not to others? Were we right in saying so before I was condemned to die, and has it now become apparent that we were talking at random and arguing for the sake of argument, and that it was really nothing but playful nonsense? I am anxious, Crito, to examine our former argument with your help, and to see whether my present circumstance will appear to me to have affected its truth in any way or not; and whether we are to set it aside, or to yield assent to it. Those of us who thought at all seriously always used to say, I think, exactly what I said just now, namely, that we ought to respect some of the opinions which men form, and not others. Tell me, Crito, I beg you, do you not think that they were right? For you in all probability will not have to die tomorrow, and your judgment will not be biased by that circumstance. Reflect, then, do you not think it reasonable to say that we should not respect all the opinions of men but only some, nor the opinions of all men but only of some men? What do you think? Is not this true?

Crito. It is.

Socr. And we should respect the good opinions, and not the worthless ones?

Crito. Yes.

Socr. But the good opinions are those of the wise, and the worthless ones those of the foolish?

Crito. Of course.

VII   *Socr.* And what did we say about this? Does a man who is in training, and who is serious about it, pay attention to the praise and blame and opinion of all men, or only of the one man who is a doctor or a trainer?

Crito. He pays attention only to the opinion of the one man.

Socr. Then he ought to fear the blame and welcome the praise of this one man, not of the multitude?

Crito. Clearly.

Socr. Then he must act and exercise, and eat and drink in whatever way the one man who is his director, and who understands the matter, tells him; not as others tell him?

Crito. That is so.

Socr. Good. But if he disobeys this one man, and disregards his opinion and his praise, and respects instead what the many say, who understand nothing of the matter, will he not suffer for it?

Crito. Of course he will.

Socr. And how will he suffer? In what way and in what part of himself?

Crito. Of course in his body. That is disabled.

Socr. You are right. And, Crito, to be brief, is it not the same in everything? And, therefore, in questions of justice and injustice, and of the base and the honorable, and of good and evil, which we are now examining, ought we to follow the opinion of the many and fear that, or the opinion of the one man who understands these matters (if we can find him), and feel more shame and fear before him than before all other men? For if we do not follow him, we shall corrupt and maim that part of us which, we used to say, is improved by justice and disabled by injustice. Or is this not so?

VIII   *Crito.* No, Socrates, I agree with you.

Socr. Now, if, by listening to the opinions of those who do not understand, we disable that part of us which is improved

by health and corrupted by disease, is our life worth living when
it is corrupt? It is the body, is it not?

Crito. Yes.

Socr. Is life worth living with the body corrupted and
crippled?

Crito. No, certainly not.

Socr. Then is life worth living when that part of us which
is maimed by injustice and benefited by justice is corrupt? Or
do we consider that part of us, whatever it is, which has to do with
justice and injustice to be of less consequence than our body?   48

Crito. No, certainly not.

Socr. But more valuable?

Crito. Yes, much more so.

Socr. Then, my good friend, we must not think so much of
what the many will say of us; we must think of what the one
man who understands justice and injustice, and of what truth herself will say of us. And so you are mistaken, to begin with, when
you invite us to regard the opinion of the multitude concerning the
just and the honorable and the good, and their opposites. But,
it may be said, the multitude can put us to death?

Crito. Yes, that is evident. That may be said, Socrates.

Socr. True. But, my good friend, to me it appears that
the conclusion which we have just reached is the same as our
conclusion of former times. Now consider whether we still hold
to the belief that we should set the highest value, not on living,
but on living well?

Crito. Yes, we do.

Socr. And living well and honorably and justly mean the
same thing: do we hold to that or not?

Crito. We do.

Socr. Then, starting from these premises, we have to con-   IX
sider whether it is just or not for me to try to escape from
prison, without the consent of the Athenians. If we find that it is
just, we will try; if not, we will give up the idea. I am afraid
that considerations of expense, and of reputation, and of bringing up my children, of which you talk, Crito, are only the

opinions of the many, who casually put men to death, and who would, if they could, as casually bring them to life again, without a thought. But reason, which is our guide, shows us that we can have nothing to consider but the question which I asked just now—namely, shall we be acting justly if we give money and thanks to the men who are to aid me in escaping, and if we ourselves take our respective parts in my escape? Or shall we in truth be acting unjustly if we do all this? And if we find that we should be acting unjustly, then we must not take any account either of death, or of any other evil that may be the consequence of remaining here, where we are, but only of acting unjustly.

Crito. I think that you are right, Socrates. But what are we to do?

Socr. Let us examine this question together, my friend, and if you can contradict anything that I say, do so, and I shall be persuaded. But if you cannot, do not go on repeating to me any longer, my dear friend, that I should escape without the consent of the Athenians. I am very anxious to act with your approval and consent. I do not want you to think me mistaken. But now tell me if you agree with the premise from which I
49 start, and try to answer my questions as you think best.

Crito. I will try.

X   *Socr.* Ought we never to act unjustly voluntarily? Or may we act unjustly in some ways, and not in others? Is it the case, as we have often agreed in former times, that it is never either good or honorable to act unjustly? Or have all our former conclusions been overturned in these few days; and did we at our age fail to recognize all along, when we were seriously conversing with each other, that we were no better than children? Is not what we used to say most certainly the truth, whether the multitude agrees with us or not? Is not acting unjustly evil and shameful in every case, whether we incur a heavier or a lighter punishment as the consequence? Do we believe that?

Crito. We do.

Socr. Then we ought never to act unjustly?

Crito. Certainly not.

Socr. If we ought never to act unjustly at all, ought we to repay injustice with injustice, as the multitude thinks we may?

Crito. Clearly not.

Socr. Well, then, Crito, ought we to do evil to anyone?

Crito. Certainly I think not, Socrates.

Socr. And is it just to repay evil with evil, as the multitude thinks, or unjust?

Crito. Certainly it is unjust.

Socr. For there is no difference, is there, between doing evil to a man and acting unjustly?

Crito. True.

Socr. Then we ought not to repay injustice with injustice or to do harm to any man, no matter what we may have suffered from him. And in conceding this, Crito, be careful that you do not concede more than you mean. For I know that only a few men hold, or ever will hold, this opinion. And so those who hold it and those who do not have no common ground of argument; they can of necessity only look with contempt on each other's belief. Do you therefore consider very carefully whether or not you agree with me and share my opinion. Are we to start in our inquiry from the premise that it is never right either to act unjustly, or to repay injustice with injustice, or to avenge ourselves on any man who harms us, by harming him in return? Or do you disagree with me and dissent from my premise? I myself have believed in it for a long time, and I believe in it still. But if you differ in any way, explain to me how. If you still hold to our former opinion, listen to my next point.

Crito. Yes, I hold to it, and I agree with you. Go on.

Socr. Then, my next point, or rather my next question, is this: Ought a man to carry out his just agreements, or may he shuffle out of them?

Crito. He ought to carry them out.

Socr. Then consider. If I escape without the state's consent, shall I be injuring those whom I ought least to injure, or not? Shall I be abiding by my just agreements or not?

Crito. I cannot answer your question, Socrates. I do not understand it.

Socr. Consider it in this way. Suppose the laws and the commonwealth were to come and appear to me as I was preparing to run away (if that is the right phrase to describe my escape) and were to ask, "Tell us, Socrates, what have you in your mind to do? What do you mean by trying to escape but to destroy us, the laws and the whole state, so far as you are able? Do you think that a state can exist and not be overthrown, in which the decisions of law are of no force, and are disregarded and undermined by private individuals?" How shall we answer questions like that, Crito? Much might be said, especially by an orator, in defense of the law which makes judicial decisions supreme. Shall I reply, "But the state has injured me by judging my case unjustly?" Shall we say that?

Crito. Certainly we will, Socrates.

XII　　　*Socr.* And suppose the laws were to reply, "Was that our agreement? Or was it that you would abide by whatever judgments the state should pronounce?" And if we were surprised by their words, perhaps they would say, "Socrates, don't be surprised by our words, but answer us; you yourself are accustomed to ask questions and to answer them. What complaint have you against us and the state, that you are trying to destroy us? Are we not, first of all, your parents? Through us your father took your mother and brought you into the world. Tell us, have you any fault to find with those of us that are the laws of marriage?" "I have none," I should reply. "Or have you any fault to find with those of us that regulate the raising of the child and the education which you, like others, received? Did we not do well in telling your father to educate you in music and athletics?" "You did," I should say. "Well, then, since you were brought into the world and raised and educated by us, how, in the first place, can you deny that you are our child and our slave, as your fathers were before you? And if this be so, do you think that your rights are on a level with ours? Do you think that you have a right to retaliate if we should try to do anything to you? You had not the same rights that your father had, or that your master would have had if you had been a slave. You had no right to retaliate if they ill-treated you, or to answer them if they scolded you, or to strike them back 51 if they struck you, or to repay them evil with evil in any way. And do you think that you may retaliate in the case of your country and its laws? If we try to destroy you, because we think it just, will you in return do all that you can to destroy us, the laws, and your country, and say that in so doing you are acting justly —you, the man who really thinks so much of excellence? Or are you too wise to see that your country is worthier, more to be revered, more sacred, and held in higher honor both by the gods and by all men of understanding, than your father and your mother and all your other ancestors; and that you ought to reverence it, and to submit to it, and to approach it more humbly when it is angry with you than you would approach your father; and either to do whatever it tells you to do or to persuade it to excuse you; and to obey in silence if it orders you to endure flogging or imprisonment, or if it sends you to battle to be wounded or to die? That is just. You must not give way, nor retreat, nor desert your station. In war, and in the court of justice, and everywhere, you must do whatever your state and your country tell you to do, or you must persuade them that their commands are unjust. But it is impious to use violence against your father or your mother; and much more impious to use violence against your country." What answer shall we make, Crito? Shall we say that the laws speak the truth, or not?

Crito. I think that they do.

Socr. "Then consider, Socrates," perhaps they would say, XIII "if we are right in saying that by attempting to escape you are attempting an injustice. We brought you into the world, we raised you, we educated you, we gave you and every other citizen a share of all the good things we could. Yet we proclaim that if any man of the Athenians is dissatisfied with us, he may take his goods and go away wherever he pleases; we give that privilege to every man who chooses to avail himself of it, so soon as he has reached manhood, and sees us, the laws, and the administration of our state. No one of us stands in his way or forbids him to take his goods and go wherever he likes, whether it be to an Athenian colony or to any foreign country, if he is dissatisfied with us and with the state. But we say that every man of you who remains here, seeing how we administer justice, and how we govern the state in other matters, has agreed, by the very fact of remaining here, to do whatsoever we tell him. And, we say, he who disobeys us acts unjustly on three counts: he disobeys us who are his parents, and he disobeys us who reared him, and he disobeys us after he has agreed to obey us, without persuading us that we are wrong. Yet we did not tell him sternly to do whatever we told him. We offered him an alternative; we gave him his choice either to obey us or to convince us that we were wrong; but he does neither.

XIV   "These are the charges, Socrates, to which we say that you will expose yourself if you do what you intend; and you are more exposed to these charges than other Athenians." And if I were to ask, "Why?" they might retort with justice that I have bound myself by the agreement with them more than other Athenians. They would say, "Socrates, we have very strong evidence that you were satisfied with us and with the state. You would not have been content to stay at home in it more than other Athenians unless you had been satisfied with it more than they. You never went away from Athens to the festivals, nor elsewhere except on military service; you never made other journeys like other men; you had no desire to see other states or other laws; you were contented with us and our state; so strongly did you prefer us, and agree to be governed by us. And what is more, you had children in this city, you found it so satisfactory. Besides, if you had wished, you might at your trial have offered to go into exile. At that time you could have done with the state's consent what you are trying now to do without it. But then you gloried in being willing to die. You said that you preferred death to exile. And now you do not honor those words: you do not respect us, the laws, for you are trying to destroy us; and you are acting just as a miserable slave would act, trying to run away, and breaking the contracts and agreement which you made to live as our citizen. First, therefore, answer this question. Are we right, or are we wrong, in saying that you have agreed not in mere words, but in your actions, to live under our government?" What are we to say, Crito? Must we not admit that it is true?

Crito. We must, Socrates.

Socr. Then they would say, "Are you not breaking your contracts and agreements with us? And you were not led to make them by force or by fraud. You did not have to make up your mind in a hurry. You had seventy years in which you might have gone away if you had been dissatisfied with us, or if the agreement had seemed to you unjust. But you preferred neither Sparta nor Crete, though you are fond of saying that they are well governed, nor any other state, either of the Greeks or the Barbarians. You went away from Athens less than the lame and the blind and the crippled. Clearly you, far more than other Athenians, were satisfied with the state, and also with us who are its laws; for who would be satisfied with a state which had no laws? And now will you not abide by your agreement? If you take our advice, you will, Socrates; then you will not make yourself ridiculous by going away from Athens. 53

"Reflect now. What good will you do yourself or your friends by thus transgressing and breaking your agreement? It is tolerably certain that they, on their part, will at least run the risk of exile, and of losing their civil rights, or of forfeiting their property. You yourself might go to one of the neighboring states, to Thebes or to Megara, for instance—for both of them are well governed—but, Socrates, you will come as an enemy to these governments, and all who care for their city will look askance at you, and think that you are a subverter of law. You will confirm the judges in their opinion, and make it seem that their verdict was a just one. For a man who is a subverter of law may well be supposed to be a corrupter of the young and thoughtless. Then will you avoid well-governed states and civilized men? Will life be worth having, if you do? Will you associate with such men, and converse without shame—about what, Socrates? About the things which you talk of here? Will you tell XV them that excellence and justice and institutions and law are the most valuable things that men can have? And do you not think that that will be a disgraceful thing for Socrates? You ought to think so. But you will leave these places; you will go to the friends of Crito in Thessaly. For there is found the greatest disorder and license, and very likely they will be delighted to hear of the ludicrous way in which you escaped from prison, dressed up in peasant's clothes, or in some other disguise which people put on when they are running away, and with your appearance altered. But will no one say how you, an old man, with probably only a few more years to live, clung so greedily to life that you dared to break the highest laws? Perhaps not, if you do not annoy them. But if you do, Socrates, you will hear much that will make you blush. You will pass your life as the flatterer and the slave of all men; and what will you be doing but feasting in Thessaly?[3] It will be as if you had made a journey to Thessaly for a banquet. And where will be all our old arguments about

54   justice and excellence then? But you wish to live for the sake of your children? You want to bring them up and educate them? What? Will you take them with you to Thessaly, and bring them up and educate them there? Will you make them strangers to their own country, that you may bestow this benefit of exile on them too? Or supposing that you leave them in Athens, will they be brought up and educated better if you are alive, though you are not with them? Yes, your friends will take care of them. Will your friends take care of them if you make a journey to Thessaly, and not if you make a journey to Hades? You ought not to think that, at least if those who call themselves your friends are worth anything at all.

XVI   "No, Socrates, be persuaded by us who have reared you. Think neither of children nor of life, nor of any other thing before justice, so that when you come to the other world you may be able to make your defense before the rulers who sit in judgment there. It is clear that neither you nor any of your friends will be happier, or juster, or more pious in this life, if you do this

---

[3] The Athenians disdained the Thessalians as heavy eaters and drinkers.—Ed.

thing, nor will you be happier after you are dead. Now you will go away a victim of the injustice, not of the laws, but of men. But if you repay evil with evil, and injustice with injustice in this shameful way, and break your agreements and covenants with us, and injure those whom you should least injure, yourself and your friends and your country and us, and so escape, then we shall be angry with you while you live, and when you die our brothers, the laws in Hades, will not receive you kindly; for they will know that on earth you did all that you could to destroy us. Listen then to us, and let not Crito persuade you to do as he says."

Be sure, my dear friend Crito, that this is what I seem   XVII
to hear, as the worshippers of Cybele seem, in their passion, to hear the music of flutes; and the sound of these arguments rings so loudly in my ears, that I cannot hear any other arguments. And I feel sure that if you try to change my mind you will speak in vain. Nevertheless, if you think that you will succeed, speak.

Crito. I have nothing more to say, Socrates.

Socr. Then let it be, Crito, and let us do as I say, since the god is our guide.

PHAEDO

The Death Scene

CHARACTERS [1]

SOCRATES   PHAEDO

CRITO   ECHECRATES

APOLLODORUS

THE SERVANT OF THE ELEVEN

THE EXECUTIONER

SCENE—The Prison of Socrates

When he had finished speaking, Crito said, "Well, Socrates,
LXIV have you any instructions for your friends or for me about your children or about anything else? How can we best serve you?"

"Simply by doing what I always tell you, Crito. Take care of your own selves, and you will serve me and mine and yourselves in all that you do, even though you make no promises now. But if you are careless of your own selves, and will not follow the path of life which we have pointed out in our conversations both today and at other times, all your promises now, however profuse and earnest they are, will be of no avail."

"We will do our best," said Crito. "But how shall we bury you?"

"As you please," he answered, "only you must catch me first, and not let me escape you." And then he looked at us with a smile and said, "My friends, I cannot convince Crito that I

---

[1] The dialogue, of which this selection is the conclusion, is presented as Phaedo's eyewitness report to Echecrates of the last day in Socrates' life. The Eleven were the police commissioners who had charge of the Athenian prison.—Ed.

67

am the Socrates who has been conversing with you, and putting his arguments in order. He thinks that I am the body which he will presently see a corpse, and he asks how he is to bury me. All the arguments which I have used to prove that I shall not remain with you after I have drunk the poison, but that I shall go away to the happiness of the blessed—all the arguments with which I tried to comfort you and myself, have been thrown away on him. Do you therefore offer security for me to him, as he offered security for me at the trial, but in a different way. He offered security for me then that I would remain; but you must offer security to him that I shall go away when I am dead, and not remain with you. Then he will feel my death less; and when he sees my body being burnt or buried, he will not be sad because he thinks that I am suffering something terrible; and at my funeral he will not say that it is Socrates whom he is laying out, or bearing to the grave, or burying. For, dear Crito, you must know that to use words wrongly is not only a fault in itself; it also corrupts the soul. You must be of good cheer, and say that you are burying my body; and you may bury it as you please, and as you think right."

With these words he rose and went into another room to 116 bathe. Crito went with him and told us to wait. So we waited,
LXV   talking of the argument and discussing it, and then again dwelling on the greatness of the calamity which had fallen upon us; it seemed as if we were going to lose a father, and to be orphans for the rest of our life. When he had bathed, and his children had been brought to him—he had two sons quite little, and one grown up—and the women of his family were come, he spoke with them in Crito's presence, and gave them his last instructions. Then he sent the women and children away and returned to us. By that time it was near the hour of sunset, for he had been a long while within. When he came back to us from the bath he sat down, but not much was said after that. Presently the servant of The Eleven came and stood before him and said, "I know that I shall not find you unreasonable like other men, Socrates. They are angry with me and curse me when I tell them to drink the poison because the authorities order me to do it.

But I have found you all along the noblest and gentlest and best man that has ever come here; and now I am sure that you will not be angry with me, but with those who you know are responsible. And so farewell, and try to bear what must be as easily as you can; you know why I have come." With that he turned away weeping, and went out.

Socrates looked up at him, and replied, "Farewell, I will do as you say." Then he turned to us and said, "How courteous the man is! And the whole time that I have been here, he has constantly come in to see me, and sometimes he has talked to me, and has been the kindest of men; and now, how generously he weeps for me! Come, Crito, let us obey him; let the poison be brought if it is ready, and if it is not ready, let it be prepared."

Crito replied, "But, Socrates, I think that the sun is still upon the hills; it has not set. Besides, I know that other men take the poison quite late, and eat and drink heartily, and even enjoy the company of their chosen friends, after the announcement has been made. So do not hurry; there is still time."

Socrates replied, "And those whom you speak of, Crito, naturally do so; for they think that they will be the gainers by so doing. And I naturally shall not do so; for I think that I should gain nothing by drinking the poison a little later but my own con- 117 tempt for so greedily saving up a life which is already spent. So do not refuse to do as I say."

Then Crito made a sign to his slave who was standing by; LXVI and the slave went out, and after some delay returned with the man who was to give the poison, carrying it prepared in a cup. When Socrates saw him, he asked, "You understand these things, my good man, what have I to do?"

"You have only to drink this," he replied, "and to walk about until your legs feel heavy, and then lie down; and it will act of itself." With that he handed the cup to Socrates, who took it quite cheerfully, Echecrates, without trembling, and without any change of color or of feature, and looked up at the man with that fixed glance of his, and asked, "What say you to making a libation from this draught? May I, or not?" "We only prepare so much as we think sufficient, Socrates," he answered. "I understand," said

Socrates. "But I suppose that I may, and must, pray to the gods that my journey hence may be prosperous. That is my prayer; may it be granted." With these words he put the cup to his lips and drank the poison quite calmly and cheerfully. Till then most of us had been able to control our grief fairly well; but when we saw him drinking, and then finish drinking, we could do so no longer: my tears came fast in spite of myself, and I covered my face and wept for myself; it was not for him, but at my own misfortune in losing such a friend. Even before that Crito had been unable to restrain his tears, and had turned away; and Apollodorus, who had never once ceased weeping the whole time, burst into a loud wail and made us one and all break down by his sobbing, except Socrates himself. "What are you doing, my friends?" he exclaimed. "I sent away the women chiefly in order that they might not behave in this way; for I have heard that a man should die peacefully. So calm yourselves and bear up." When we heard that, we were ashamed, and we stopped weeping. But he walked about, until he said that his legs were getting heavy, and then he lay down on his back, as he was told. And the man who had given the poison after a while began to examine his feet and legs. Then he pressed his foot hard, and asked if there were any feeling in it, and Socrates said, "No"; and then his legs, and in this way moved upwards, showing us that he was cold and stiff. And again he felt him, and said that when it reached his heart, he would be gone. He was already growing cold about the groin, when he uncovered his face, which had been covered, and spoke for the last time. "Crito," he said, "I owe a cock to Asclepius;[2] do not forget it." "It shall be done," replied Crito. "Is there anything else that you wish?" He made no reply to this question; but after a moment he stirred, and the man uncovered him. His eyes were fixed. Then Crito closed his mouth and his eyes.

Such was the end, Echecrates, of our friend, who was, I think, of all the men of our time, the best, the wisest, and the most just.

[2] It was customary on recovering from sickness to offer a cock to Asclepius, the god of healing.—Ed.

118

www.ingramcontent.com/pod-product-compliance
Lightning Source LLC
LaVergne TN
LVHW011215080426
835508LV00007B/809